WHY WOMEN SHOULDN'T MARRY

WHY WOMEN SHOULDN'T MARRY

Being Single by Choice

Cynthia S. Smith *&* Hillary B. Smith

Fort Lee, New Jersey

Published by Barricade Books Inc.
185 Bridge Plaza North
Suite 308-A
Fort Lee, NJ 07024

www.barricadebooks.com

Library of Congress Cataloging-in-Publication Data
Smith, Cynthia S.
 Why women shouldn't marry / Cynthia S. Smith and Hillary B. Smith.
    p. cm.
 ISBN 978-1-56980-344-8 (pbk.)
    1. Single women--United States. 2. Marriage--United States. I. Smith,
Hillary B. II. Title.

 HQ800.2.S65 2007
 306.81'530973--dc22

                                                          2007049109

 ISBN 13: 978-1-56980-344-8
 ISBN 10: 1-56980-344-7

10 9 8 7 6 5 4 3 2 1

Manufactured in the United States of America

To our William

CONTENTS

If those are your specifications, why you should rethink your goal. THE DON'T-BREAK-YOUR-HEART CHECKLIST: WHAT NOT TO EXPECT FROM MEN. Read it and weep.

How the 1988 *Why Women Shouldn't Marry* book hit a nerve
among women and enabled them to change (and in some cases
save) their lives.

Single is no longer singular—it's just a whole new frame of reference. The numbers of women who live alone have reached
new highs. The independent single women of today are regarded with respect, not pity. Stop driving yourself nuts to find a
husband but think first: do you really want and need to get married to live a full life?

ACKNOWLEDGMENTS

WE WANT TO convey special thanks to the many women who were willing to reveal their life experiences and share their innermost feelings for this book. Their hope, and ours, is that their important contribution will serve to ease the way for every woman who has viewed herself as being alone in the conflict of single versus married.

We also want to express our appreciation to Mark Zanetti for his invaluable tech support.

PREFACE

THINGS HAVE CHANGED for women since 1988 when the original *Why Women Shouldn't Marry* was published. Take societal attitudes about marriage: Who would have thought back then that parents of young women would speak freely about their "sin-in-law," the guy who lives with their daughter? Who would have thought that women would have babies without caring about marrying the dads?

But what hasn't changed is the perennial desire for women to get married...but not all women. What still exists is the drive that pushes many of them into unfortunate marriages. Today is an era of choices for women—to marry or not, to have a career or not, to have kids or not—and those very choices can create complications and anguish.

The purpose of the updating of *Why Women Shouldn't Marry* is to help women make the right choices for them, to enable them to recognize their needs and motivations, to learn from the experiences of others when and when not to marry—at any age.

Check through the book, and read about women who may have been in your situation, and learn from their successes or failures. Single, divorced, widowed—there are reasons not to marry that you should become aware of before you make what could be the wrong decision for you.

1

YOUR LIFE...YOUR CHOICE

IF YOU'RE HEADING to the kitchen for the Häagen-Dazs after the phone call from mom pointedly reporting the upcoming nuptials of her friend's daughter—stop. Calories compound guilt, they don't assuage it. You're nearing or are past thirty. Your mother already had three children by then, and you haven't yet met any guy you'd want to spend the rest of your life with let alone be the father of your children. So what?

Today, it's your choice to remain single—as long as you want to or even forever. You're having a great time. You have a fulfilling career, a busy even hectic life filled with friends and freedom to do whatever you want, whenever you want. Maybe you'd like to get married, someday, but don't allow yourself to be pressured by the needs of others. Mom and dad want grandchildren...that's not your problem. Mom says she wants you to hurry to achieve the same fulfilling joys of marriage she has had, which is a matter of perception. You view her constantly subordinating self as antithetical to your ideas of a happy life, but she sees it as the wifely role in marriage that worked out well for her. But is that for you?

There's no question that marriage is a matter of give-and-take, but success depends on just how much each partner is willing to do. What's puzzling is all the articles about why men shouldn't marry. What on earth do they have to lose? When a man marries, he gets someone to take care of all his needs—usually a neat, well-run home, laundry, meals, sex, morale boosting, cheerleading, a companion plus another paycheck. What does the woman get?

When Cynthia was researching the book *The Seven Levels of Marriage* a number of years ago, one of the questions posed in all male interviews was: "Who gives the most in your marriage?" Ninety-two percent of men queried answered immediately, "My wife" and frequently gave a figure—"She's 80 percent, and I'm 20" or numbers equally disparate.

Most of the giving and compromising involved in marriage is performed by the women. Why do we do that? Is it because we have been socialized (or brainwashed) to believe we have more to gain from the arrangement and therefore must suppress our desires and sublimate our needs in order to make him happy?

Marriage has usually been regarded in lore and law as a trap for men and a sinecure for women. As described in a current Web site called *NoMarriage.com*, "Marriage is a sham for men. There is no benefit. If you are about to get married, think it over. Don't let your dick do your thinking for you. Don't let your punch-drunk I'm in love euphoria put you on autopilot. You will wake up in a hell of a hangover staring at this woman who will control your life."

It is true that women think more about marriage than men do. Who didn't play bride when she was a girl or covet the wedding Barbie? We have been trained to be enchanted with the romantic emotional ambiance of The Wedding. As she comes down the aisle, all misty eyes turn to the cynosure of the day—the bride in perhaps the most glorious dress she will ever wear—her flowing white wedding gown. Who doesn't want to be the star of such a day...the envy of all the unmarried bridesmaids and pride of the mother who now has proven she has raised a desirable daughter? And you'll notice there are brides' magazines, but not grooms.'

When Cynthia got married many years ago, she chose to have the wedding at New York's Sherry-Netherland Hotel on Fifth Avenue, not because of the posh location, but because the ceremony involved coming down a majestic curved staircase and long aisle leading to the flowered altar. As she told her mother, "This is my day, and I want everyone to have to look at me as long as possible."

When the original version of this book was written in 1988, it was posited that the only reasons for a woman to marry were the needs for sperm or support—if she wanted children, and/or she needed the income to support her family. Today, women have children and remain in the work force, so the need for support is no longer a factor, and resident fathers are not a necessary part of the equation. More and more women are opting for single motherhood, having children alone or not remarrying after divorce.

Maybe you don't have the primal craving to be a mother. The sacrosanct dogma that all women are born with a powerful maternal instinct is now being refuted as mothers are coming out of the closet to confess that if they had it to do over again, they'd never have had children. Today, women who do not want children are no longer regarded as oddities. It was always assumed when you encountered a woman with no children that the cause was infertility, and you regarded her with pity.

Today, when dealing with the "why no kids?" query often posed by smug women who feel they are the "mothers superior," the woman with the chic midwinter tan recently acquired on the ski slopes at Aspen smilingly answers that she and her husband never wanted to have their freedom blighted by the little monsters—and she looks pityingly at the pale, worn questioner who now regards her with secret envy.

According to the definitive and highly respected "The State of Our Unions 2007," Rutgers University's study of the social health of marriage in America: "...the marital relationship today is so different from what it was in the past. Marriage is now based almost entirely on close friendship and romantic love, mostly stripped of the economic dependencies, legal and religious restrictions, and extended family pressures that have held marriages together for most of human history. Until fairly recent times marriages had little to do with romantic love, sexual passion, or even close friendship; they were functional partnerships in the intense struggle of life."

If you are fortunate enough to have a living grandmother, ask her about the details of her grandmother's marriage. In those days, marriages were arranged by parents based on their view of suitability of the match. Evaluated elements were financial stability and familial social status. Age and appearance were regarded as totally irrelevant, and often, the future bride had no say in the choice. In those days, every wife lived with a Marriage Misery Meter—the measurement of how much unhappiness she was expected to accept in the marriage. If she was lucky, they got along, but if she wasn't, emotional and physical abuse was often part of her married life.

By the next generation, couples chose their own spouses. However, since she had no means of support, the woman usually largely made her choice based on how good a provider he was, which meant the Marriage Misery Meter was still in operation: She still had to accept a certain level of unhappiness.

TODAY WE HAVE the Happiness Marriage Meter: "Does living with him make me happy?" "How much crap do I have to take in order to keep this marriage going?" "Do the pleasures of love and companionship compensate for the compromises I have to make?" The truth is that every cohabiting relationship requires dealing with the needs and desires of your partner. If you see such situations as yielding rather than just part of a partnered life and don't feel the satisfaction of giving someone you love pleasure without resenting it and feeling that the cost is too great for you, then you shouldn't marry.

We are no longer a "couples world." Women are now free to enjoy whatever lifestyles they wish, from living totally alone or in relationships either legal or informal. Whereas years ago unmarried women past thirty were regarded as virginal spinsters who spent their pathetic evenings eating microwaved dinners in front of TV, today the image is "Sex and the City" sophisticates who pass their evenings drinking wine in bed with the latest hot guys. That show has done much to remove some of the age-old demeaning sexual givens, such as that dumping and rejection are done by men only. And that single women are undesirable single ladies, and single straight men are dashing bachelors—suave, socially in demand studs described by the great misanthrope George Bernard Shaw, "A married man is a man with a past, while a bachelor is a man with a future." Never mind that the bachelor is an unappetizing-looking schnook with the personality of a comatose squid. If he isn't married, we must assume it is the choice of the dashing man-about-town who has not yet found any woman wonderful enough to seduce him away from his sybaritic existence.

If you have been widowed or divorced and already have children, what is your incentive to remarry? The famous mystery writer Dame P. D. James, who was widowed some years ago, was asked by an interviewer whether she intended to marry again. "What for?" was her answer as she went on to say that she had no intention of starting a family as she had three grown children, and that although she enjoyed male companionship for travel, dinner, and sex, there was a great pleasure in saying good-bye at the door and returning to the lovely privacy of her own home.

Once you have passed the grief of loss which overcomes widows and divorcees alike, albeit in different ways, you probably have established a highly satisfactory existence that is, for the first time in your life, totally devoted to your wants and needs. Why on earth should you allow a man to move in on you, bringing his demands and idiosyncrasies that force you to reshape your life into his image?

Since the beginning of time, women have been driven into marriage by fears of their own inadequacies, which require the ministrations and care of men in order to survive. We cannot take care of ourselves, we cannot support ourselves, we need the strength and greater wisdom and experience of men to lean upon and control our lives. In fact, we are so unworldly and incompetent that we can only be judged and valued by the achievements of our husbands and are rated only by reflections of his glories. Strangely enough, even if she had fought her way up through the mire of a man's world and had reached a position of importance, there were those (both men and women) who looked upon her with pity because she had not been able to "catch a man."

The late Wendy Wasserstein, the internationally renowned playwright, was emotionally pained all of her life by the disapproval of her mother, who saw her as a failure because she had never married. When she was awarded the Pulitzer Prize, the greatest American honor for any writer, her mother reacted not with pride, but only pity that her daughter was not as successful as her brother, who had a firm on Wall Street and a family.

Cynthia was the advertising director of a company for many years, the only female executive there. She was accepted as "one of the guys" because she was married, and it used to infuriate her to hear the men's scorn of two successful women in her industry who had never married and would be mocked, with a knowing leer, as "needing a good lay." What was really aggravating was that many women bought the whole line.

When Cynthia's husband died, one of her friends said to her at the funeral, "Not to worry, you're still young and attractive. You will marry again." The tactlessness and tastelessness of people never ceases to amaze. "Why?" Cynthia asked. The woman looked at her as though she was slightly deranged. "Why, you must have a man to take care of you, of course." Since in all the marriages she had observed, caretaking was the woman's department, Cynthia asked truly puzzled, "What must he take care of?" In total surprise, the friend answered in her best *cela va sans dire* voice, "Why, to take care of money, to pay the bills, to take care of the car, to take out the garbage [that one Cynthia bought]—you know, all those things the man of the family does."

Aha, all that important stuff that we fluffy-headed females have been taught are beyond our competence. The sort of things Cynthia's father did for fifty-two years and her mother learned to do within two months after he died. The onerous tasks Cynthia performed in her thirty-five-year marriage because her husband was a graphic designer and even worse at math than she was. The simple responsibilities assumed today by millions of single women as routine chores. Years ago he brought home the bacon, and she cooked it. But today either one does it—depending upon who does it better.

So why do you need a husband? (And how many a single woman who comes home exhausted from work would love to have a wife?) Women no longer have to marry in order to achieve happiness, and to not be a wife is a viable and personal choice—yours.

Why should you marry? What will you really get out of it, and what will you give up? Is it worth changing your life, perhaps not for the better, just to acquire the title of Mrs., which many women have dropped in favor of Ms.? Once you begin to weigh the compensations against the concessions, the bonds of matrimony may get to look more constrictive than constructive.

Millions of women today are making the decision to stay single and love it. This is the era of choice. You should not marry simply because it's been the accepted woman's role for centuries. Women should not permit themselves to be shoved into molds that do not suit them and engender their unhappiness and discontent. Today, you do not have to live a life of anyone else's choosing but yours.

HERE'S WHY YOU SHOULDN'T MARRY

WHEN THE FIRST version of this book came out and was discussed on TV and radio shows, the inevitable interviewer-to-author question was: "Don't you believe in marriage? Your book tells women not to marry!"

The answer always was: "This book does not tell women not to marry—but not to marry for the wrong reasons."

Gender roles in society have changed radically within recent years. In fact, there are no longer any differences—women are now active and fully accepted in the worlds of politics, business, and science. Their ambitions can now take them far away from the limitations of wife, homemaker, and mother.

In his essay in Rutgers's "The State of Our Unions 2007," Dr. Paul Popenoe posits that long-term trends point to the gradual weakening of marriage as the primary social institution of family life. He also points to a shift toward faith in personal independence and tolerance for diverse lifestyles—otherwise known as "secular individualism."

The purpose of this book is to help guide women through the complex choices never before available to them and ensure that they make lifestyle selections based on current rather than outdated mores.

THE "WHY YOU SHOULDN'T MARRY" GUIDE

Mom and Dad never miss a chance to needle you. "So when?"
You made the mistake of bringing a guy home for Thanksgiving, Christmas, Passover, whatever, and mom and dad loved him. "He's nice looking, he's an engineer, he's polite—what more do you want?" And the inevitable little dig, "You're not getting any younger, you know." In the "old days," bringing home a boyfriend to meet the family was not considered a casual event, but was tantamount to an engagement. Perhaps the guy you see as just a friend your parents view as a possible suitor. Either enlighten mom and dad or cut out the hospitality.

Two of your best friends just got married.
You caught the bouquet both times. And you're sick of being a bridesmaid and having to lay out big bucks for some god-awful dresses that match the wedding color schemes but make you look like death. If everybody's doing it, maybe…

Your live-in significant other keeps pestering you to tie the knot.
He's charming, but is not exactly a ball of fire in the income-making department. His small antique-toy shop is only open days when he's not off on buying trips. He claims he's just a simple guy who enjoys the simple pleasures, but sure revels in the luxuries supplied by your lavish annual income. His laid-back attitude, a common euphemism for lack of ambition, bothers the hell out of you.

You really want to have kids, and you think he'd make a great dad.
The primary role is husband. If that doesn't work, then parenting becomes a painful disaster.

He makes megabucks.
He can assure you a house in the Hamptons, a Soho condo, skiing in the Alps, and other upscale goodies. Your profession is prestigious and gratifying, but strictly middle class incomewise. A rich husband is lovely, but wealth is not always permanent (witness the Wall Street whizzes who have ended up in the Allenwood federal pen). You should never marry a man for what he has, but only what he is.

You are beginning to wonder if maybe you are being too fussy.
You've had a number of boyfriends over the years, even lived with a few, and the one who shares your apartment now is quite lovable and nice. Your biological clock is ticking louder and louder. So maybe he's the one.

You think it's time.
Marriage is not like musical chairs—you don't settle into one because it's the one that happens to be handy.

You will have to lose yourself to make a marriage work.

Take a good look...are you truly yourself when you are with him?

You want to be taken care of.

Dependence breeds contempt by him and ultimately contempt for yourself for surrendering who you are for a specious prize, "Security."

2

WHERE DID THEIR FREEDOM COME FROM?

HILLARY JUST WENT to a baby shower for a twenty-five-year-old woman. All seemed pretty much as expected. The house was decorated with balloons and ribbons, and a table was overflowing with presents. The proud expectant parents showed their guests the nursery and all the expectant grandparents were there beaming. OK, what has this got to do with this book?

The mother-to-be was not married, and no one cared, except maybe the expectant father, who contrary to the old image of shotgun weddings where the guy was forced at gunpoint to marry the girl he had impregnated, couldn't persuade the mother of his coming child to set a date. She was in no hurry to marry. Actually, the thought of it didn't seem to figure at all in her life decisions. She earned a good living, had bought her house several years before, and was now having a baby. She had everything. One got the feeling that the expectant father was feeling somewhat insecure because he wasn't sure how much he was needed now or later.

Here's what was amazing. Thirty years ago when Hillary was a young woman, her generation died a thousand emotional deaths over the desire to "have it all." They believed the feminists, but they suffered because deep down, they weren't yet sure they or society would really accept the reality of "liberated women." Now, this young woman just took it all for granted. She was forging ahead on her own terms without a thought of marriage. Did she and her peers realize how hard won all this freedom of choice was?

Has the promise of feminism become so well integrated into our society that young people seem unaware of the origins of the benefits earned for them? The women of the Baby Boom generation were the guineas pigs in a grand social experiment called feminism. Betty Friedan wrote *The Feminine Mystique*, and the underpinnings of a generation raised to become June Cleaver were changed forever. Gloria Steinem started a magazine called *Ms.*, thus popularizing a title for all women that became accepted at amazing speed.

They set out to do it all and have it all, as promised. In the late sixties and seventies, they went to college and then to graduate school. They were no longer coeds looking for husbands. They believed they could be as effective in the workplace as a man and pursued their education and careers accordingly. Not nurses, but doctors. Not legal secretaries, but lawyers. But at what cost? The idea was all right, but for three things: the glass ceiling at work, the resentment of their male counterparts (and romantic partners), and last but not least, that doleful ticking of their biological clocks.

The paradox of the time and the burden carried by all of these women was that deep down, they still wanted the June Cleaver life—the husband, the 2.5 kids, and the house in the suburbs—as they had been brought up to desire. Sure, now they could buy the house themselves, but these educated, worldly women found they still had a foot in the prefeminist life and for the most part wanted children and fathers to live in that house with them. For that, they needed husbands, and that was when all the rhetoric of feminism came crashing down. The drive to be married strangled the lives of these independent women, and so many women Baby Boomers ended up wanting to get married in the worst way—and did.

So when Hillary attended that baby shower with the total unconcern for biological clocks, or need for marriage, she felt quietly proud of their contribution, a little jealous, and not a little sad at the tragedy of her generation. They paid the price for your progress. So say thank you!

WHY SHOULD I?

WHEN SHE WALKED in, she could have stepped right out of the TV screen...tall and slender; long, straight, light-blonde hair; bright blue eyes; and a smile that looked like an ad for teeth whitener. Dressed in casual jeans and white shirt, slight but with seemly cleavage, Samantha looked like one of today's conventional stunners—until she laughed and you saw the gold bead embedded in her tongue.

Samantha has always lived life on her own terms. Self-confident, achieving, and single at thirty, she has two degrees and is now studying for her Ph.D. in English literature with the goal of becoming part of university academia. She supports herself by working more than one job in order to feed her soul as well as her body. During the week, she teaches classes to young unwed mothers, and on weekends, she has a very lucrative job as a bartender in a busy downtown establishment. She owns her own house, is financially very responsible, always keeping three months ahead of all her bills, and travels a good deal. She had just returned from a trip to Costa Rica, Peru, Guatemala, and Mexico.

When we asked her if she wants to get married, she answered without hesitation and without affect, "If it happens—OK. If it doesn't—OK, also."

There was no need to ask if she'd had boyfriends, just how many.

"I have a lot of friends," she said. "Men are not important, people are."

Had she ever been in love?

Yes, and she had crossed country to move in with him. It had lasted a while until she felt he was not one with whom she wanted to share her life. "He would spend Sundays—every Sunday—in front of TV watching football. I wanted to go out, hiking, walking, going to theater, doing things. He resisted." Finally, she felt he was, as she put it, "Just violating my personal space." And she left.

The "my own space" concept has been heard now for many years and was the bane of every woman whose boyfriend used the hated term to terminate a relationship. But Samantha uses it freely in a different way, perhaps in the purest sense. She has a strong self; who she is and what she wants is paramount. Anyone or thing that interferes with that drive is impinging on and interfering with the life she is building for herself. And she just won't have it.

Samantha is fortunate in having parents who do not pressure her to marry or change her lifestyle in any way. She likes her parents and enjoys visiting them—they live nearby. When asked if her lack of interest in marriage came about from the state of her parents' relationship, she shook her head and seemed even surprised by the question. "They're fine. They've been married for thirty-seven years, for goodness sakes!" As though longevity defines success.

Samantha is a good person with strong direction and absolutely none of that nauseating sense of entitlement that fills so many young people today. Because she expects little from anyone but herself, she has the great asset of being self-actualized.

Today, the one major reason women say they want to or need to marry is to have children.

"Would you get married to have children?" she was asked. She looked stunned at the question. "Absolutely not. I don't want to have babies. If I should at some time in the years ahead decide I want to be a mother, I'll adopt."

But you got the feeling that being a mother would be too demanding and would certainly "violate her personal space." She proves the point that all women do not have the powerful maternal urge—a role that was assigned to them by the years of brainwashing by men who told them they were not qualified or capable of doing anything else. Today's woman is not held back from doing or being anything she wants—and Samantha is the perfect example of why women do not have to marry in order to have a fulfilling and valuable life.

3

THE SOUL MATE MYTH

UNLIKE SAMANTHA, THERE is a large group of women who are mired in the great cliché of the current husband-hunting era. The Soul Mate Myth has been spread by otherwise intelligent women who don't know what the hell they're talking about and has become the excuse for avoiding marriage by some women who really do not want to be wives and by achieving young women who have an exalted and extreme view of their own elite superiority.

The actual origin of the term is a Greek myth. Zeus became angered by the bold behavior of humans and decided to punish them by cutting them in half. It seemed like a good idea at the time, but then he found it caused unexpected complications. So Zeus decided to enable each half to come together with his or her other half. As a result, every female sought her male half, and every male sought his female half, allowing them to reproduce.

That's a nice story, but the copulation population was smaller and more localized in Zeus's day. If there's only one soul mate in the universe for you, suppose he's leading mountain-climbing expeditions in Katmandu?

THE SOUL MATE CHECKLIST

WE ASKED A group of young women between the ages of twenty-five and thirty-five, all of whom are earning high incomes and want to marry, what they are looking for in a husband. Because they are financially secure, they felt that "we expect more from men than did previous generations. We're looking for more than just a provider—we're looking for a soul mate."

When we asked them to define a soul mate, here is their checklist of expectations:

He Must Be:
- A companion
- A best friend
- Someone to talk to and support me when I'm down
- Always there for me
- Ready to commit to me
- Someone who always puts me first
- Someone who loves me for who I am

Give us a break!

Notice all the requirements involve what he will give to me. And what does this superhero get in return for his devotion? Having all these splendid traits must come at a great cost to self and ego. It would be virtually impossible to find all this compassion and understanding in one person. Do you want a clone or a totally subservient schmuck?

So as long as you go on pursuing this elusive ideal, the years will pass, and you will remain single. If that's your subconscious goal, fine. But if you don't come down off your high horse and realize the impossibility of this quest, you may be inadvertently giving up your deep and real wish for marriage.

THE NEGATIVE RAMIFICATIONS OF THE SOUL MATE SEARCH

OK—YOU WON. You finally found your soul mate and married him. We can almost guarantee divorce within ten years. Why? Because perfection is not permanent: Life changes, people change. As the years go on, factors that created certain needs at one time of your life are no longer applicable. They will be altered by conflicts caused by careers, children, and Life. Your soul mate checklist was a romantic, impractical, and thoroughly unrealistic evaluation of who you are and whom you need to fulfill your dream vision of your future. But since you placed such importance on the rigid qualifications for a husband, how well will you handle the changes in his personality and behavior as his world expands beyond fulfilling your needs? And what about the quid pro quo to which he is entitled and perhaps is tired of having ignored?

The real problem with the Soul Mate Myth search is that, by undergoing repeated disappointments in your fruitless search for the ideal companion, you may well become battle weary and give up on the whole concept. Then when you do the normal thing all we mere mortals do—compromise—you may feel you have committed the cardinal single-woman sin…you have settled and actually sold short the true value of the nice guy you married.

The Soul Mate Myth is destructive because it will keep you from forming authentic relationships that have a chance to thrive instead of fail. Don't marry because you think you have found your soul mate; it is bound to buckle under the unbearable weight of expected perfection.

YOUR SOUL MATE IS PROBABLY PLURAL

BE OPEN MINDED and fair: Admit that it's hard to find everything in one neat package. Perhaps you should assign all your emotional-need fulfillments to many people—friends, parents, siblings—and not lay the entire load on one guy!

We've always had lots of close friends—some from childhood, some from college, and some acquired more recently. When one of us decides we need to talk to someone about a problem, we decide with whom to have this discussion. It may be we'll pick up the phone and call each other, or it may be someone else whom we feel will relate better to the problem, who will be the most empathetic and will give the best advice.

Remember—we now live in an era of specialization. Take advantage of the value of the concept, and split the demands of your soul mate role among many.

THE DON'T-BREAK-YOUR-HEART CHECKLIST OF WHAT NOT TO EXPECT FROM MEN

FACE IT, THEY'RE different. So don't waste your time looking for qualities they just don't have. Men are not bad. They can be wonderful friends, companions, and lovers, as long as you don't expect what they are unable to provide or do.

Do Not Expect of Him:

- Heart-to-heart discussions about your relationship
- Calling you the next day or week
- If you have kids, liking or even tolerating your teenagers
- Listening endlessly to details about your problems and job
- Always being sympathetic and supportive about your concerns
- Complimenting you on your new hairdo and noticing your new dress
- Understanding why you get angry when he puts a golf or poker game ahead of you
- Telling you you look thin in those jeans

4

WHO NEEDS A "HE" WHEN I HAVE ME?

AN ENGLISH PROFESSOR wrote this sentence on the black-board and asked his students to punctuate it correctly:

"A woman without her man is nothing."

All the males in the class wrote:

"A woman, without her man, is nothing."

All the females in the class wrote:

"A woman: without her, man is nothing."

EMOTIONAL SHORTCHANGING

WHEN TWO PEOPLE live together, there has to be some sort of quid pro quo emotionally or they're just roommates. However, emotional needs vary, and some people have higher thresholds of need than others. People who care for each other usually become aware of these thresholds because love carries with it the desire to make each other happy. Most of the time, this is not difficult when dealing with only mundane details. But the true test of a good relationship is when each person is willing to accept a certain amount of inconvenience, or even unhappiness, in order to please the other. Unfortunately, that old macho ego gets in the way of good judgment in such situations, and although the man claims to see the couple as equal, he really believes the male is more equal. Any threat to his perceived superiority, and thus greater needs, is unacceptable. In previous generations, women went along with such dicta. But no more.

Amy hung up the phone, and her friend, Mary, noting the familiar look of annoyance and anger, said, "Not another of those 'We'd-better-stop-seeing-each-other-because-I'm-getting-to-like-you-too-much-and-I-don't-want-to-get-married-yet-so-this-is-the-wrong-time' calls?"

Amy nodded, flopped into a chair and said disgustedly, "What makes that yo-yo think I want to marry him or anybody else for that matter right now?"

If a young woman said that forty years ago, the statement would have been regarded as sour grapes or stupidity. Which girl didn't want to become "Mrs." and have a husband, home, and family, live in the affluent style that it was hoped his growing ambition would provide for the rest of her life? How else could a woman's success be measured?

If she was unfortunate enough to remain single, it was universally accepted that this was not out of choice, but because she was unlovable and unlovely. Way back in the 1930s, many of the commonly prevalent unmarried lady teachers were rumored to have lost "sweethearts" in the Big War. No one ever knew who spread those rumors, but it is quite possible it was they themselves in order to convey an image of romantic tragedy rather than pathetic rejection and to mitigate the ugly epithet of "old maid."

One would be hard pressed to reconcile the cliché image of an "old maid" with thirty-six-year-old Amy. Instead of sensible shoes and shapeless print dresses, she wears Reeboks and jeans. Any resemblance to the prim-crimped spinster of yore is entirely forgotten when you see this trim blonde woman who exudes vitality.

Amy grew up in a middle-class home in a suburb of a major city, the only child of intelligent, loving parents. She went off to Bennington College for a fine-arts degree and returned home until she found a job in her chosen field, whereupon she moved into her own apartment.

"I love my job and my life. I have lots of friends, men and women. There's always lots to do and people to do it with. Sure, I sort of expect to get married someday, but that so-called right someone just hasn't materialized. Maybe because I don't really need a husband the way women did years ago. I've been moving along in my career, making more and more money, and getting a big kick out of spending it freely. I've enjoyed furnishing my apartment just the way I like. I hear married friends arguing with husbands over every stick of furniture. I've picked out every piece carefully, it's my home, my taste, and I love it. I buy clothes whenever I want without having to justify the bills to anyone. I'm free to travel on my own, unencumbered by the pulls of a partner. I go when and where I want. I'm totally free, and it's unbeatable. I have nothing against marriage, but as I see it now, how will it improve my life?"

Amy has had a number of relationships over the years, and each time, there was a possibility of culmination in marriage that just never worked out. Then she met Tom, an accountant with whom she fell deeply in love.

They saw each other constantly until it made sense to live together. Since she had the larger apartment, he moved in. The first few months were heavenly. Tom had a good job with a large accounting firm, and Amy was happy in her position. They enjoyed cooking dinner together, shopping together, jogging, playing tennis, and meeting with friends. Tom was loving and caring and romantic. From time to time, he would surprise her with little gifts, and Amy's feelings for him were becoming deeper and deeper. The strong sexual passion of their relationship had developed into something warm and wonderful as each cared and learned to please each other.

"At last," Amy thought, "I've finally met the man I want to marry and spend the rest of my life with." Then one day, Amy received a call in her office offering her the coveted position of head of the city's cultural arts center, a job that would offer not only tremendous responsibility and a significant salary increase, but high public visibility and the chance to become part of the top echelon of the city's movers and shakers. It was the opportunity of a lifetime and she couldn't wait to get home to share her wonderful news with Tom and talk over the myriad ways this new career could change their lives. She found him in the kitchen. Their arrangement had always been whoever got home first started dinner. Amy tossed her bag and attaché case on the table and began to regale him excitedly with the details of her new job.

"Imagine, I'm going to be the administrator of all the arts activities of this city! I'll be responsible for the coordination of the ballet, symphony and opera performances at the Fine Arts Center. That means booking performers, arranging for funding, working with the producers, directors, and artists." Her voice trailed off as she realized that Tom had not said one word or registered any response to her enthusiastic outpouring, but merely continued to chop and slice onions, mushrooms, and other ingredients for a stir-fry dinner.

"Don't you think it's a fantastic opportunity?" she asked somewhat tentatively.

"Sure," he said, "if you like to be an ass-licking whore to a bunch of rich people. All you'll really be is a glorified fund-raiser sucking up to the town muck-mucks for contributions. What's the big deal?" Then he strode past her to open the fridge, where he began rummaging through the shelves.

Amy felt as though she had been kicked in the stomach. In one cruel blow, he had managed to douse her enthusiasm and strip her of her self-esteem. How can someone be so hurtful, let alone to someone you profess to love? Here she was proud of being selected for this dream job and thrilled with the possibilities it promised, and he made her feel like a naïve, unperceptive idiot. Even if he thought she was overreacting and endowing the position with unrealistic advantages, wouldn't it have been kinder to initially greet her exultation with congratulations and then follow up later with a discussion about what he viewed as the realities?

She went into the bedroom to change into her evening outfit of jeans and T-shirt, and her eyes filled with tears. Amy realized that perhaps Tom was either envious or threatened by this change in her career status. She longed to talk it out with him, but was put off by his closed, silent face at dinner followed by his refusal to look up from TV football for the rest of the evening. She found herself resenting that he deprived her of the tremendous pleasure of anticipating the joys the new job promised.

So she did what she had always done before Tom. She called her friend, Mary, and enjoyed an hour phone chat and Mary's screams of delight as they talked about the wonderful people she would be meeting, the parties and galas she would be organizing and attending, the great fun of having a leading part in the thrilling world of the arts. Mary pointed out how this upward move would place Amy in a new career level that would surely ensure her future. It was the kind of conversation Amy had expected to have had with Tom.

The ensuing months were filled with exciting events and immersion in a totally new world of artists, civic leaders, and officials, all of whom regarded Amy as a respected peer. Work was a joy, but home was hell. The reasons for Tom's initial adverse reaction became obvious as his jealousy manifested itself in offensive and petty ways. There was a constant stream of snide remarks about her being nothing but a foolish foil for the tax-saving tactics of the rich.

It was true that part of Amy's job consisted of fund-raising that required attending charity balls and dinner parties to mingle with the moneyed people who could give large donations to the arts. To an attractive vivacious woman like Amy, this was one of the big perks of her position, and she hated Tom's attempts to mock these gala fun activities as demeaning moneygrubbing chores. She understood what demons drove him to take this tack, but knowledge did not make his relentless criticism and digs any more palatable.

Amy tried to talk with him about his feelings, but he was impossible to reach. Like most men, Tom had great difficulty in talking about his feelings. In their book *Why Can't Men Open Up?* authors Steven Naifeh and Gregory White Smith state, "We're raised to be closed men. By closing ourselves to feelings, we thought we could escape the anxieties and disappointments of emotional involvement."

Amy tried to think how she would feel if Tom outdistanced her professionally. Would she be as jealous and odious? She concluded that she might feel a stab of envy here and there, but on the whole she would be happy for and proud of him. Tom professed to be a modern man who viewed women as equals, and he was fine as long as Amy and he were equal. What he couldn't accept was when she became more than equal. Like many men who view themselves as liberal antitheses to male chauvinists, he was comfortable until challenged. Tom's anger and frustration alarmingly began to spill over from abuse at home to irate calls to Amy's office when she worked late and rude demands of her secretary to locate Amy immediately whenever he wanted to discuss some minor matter. His harassing behavior became insufferable and unsupportable.

Amy's job was a high-powered one that involved lots of stress: endless meetings, dealing with many crises, and handling many temperaments. She reveled in her power and the approval she received from all her superiors. Many evenings she would arrive home exhausted and want nothing more than a quiet dinner, some TV, and bed. There were many times when she did not want to talk at all, but just needed privacy and solitude. Instead, she would be met by a hostile Tom who demanded to know what had occurred during her day so that he could point out what she had done wrong and disparage her performance and position. She remembered an aphorism that a true friend is not one who sympathizes with your sorrows and misfortune, but one who shares and admires your successes and good fortune. She realized that she was seeing a side of him that she never knew existed.

Finally, one evening after a particularly brutal confrontation with Tom, Amy asked herself, "What do I need this for? What am I getting out of this relationship except aggravation?" She loved her job and the new world in which she had become a respected participant. She realized that much of the potential pleasure she could be enjoying was being destroyed by the need to tiptoe around Tom's sensitive psyche to avoid being debased. She became aware that his constant emotional abuse had changed their relationship; their sex life was all but gone, as it was hard to feel desire for someone who denigrated your achievements and made you feel like an inept idiot. Living together had become a misery. She no longer loved him or even liked him. This was not the man she wanted to marry. So she told him to leave.

Amy had discovered a fact that women have come to realize: True exchange of feelings and emotions is something you enjoy with women friends. Lucky is the gal whose husband or lover even listens. Too often men view women as sounding boards for their ideas and anxieties, but are unwilling or is it unable to return the favor.

Further along in their book *Why Can't Men Open Up?* Naifeh and White Smith point out that "Afraid like Ulysses to be lured by the Sirens and yield his freedom, strength and masculinity, men are bred to view feelings as feminine and silence as strength. Torn between the demands of manhood and the need for intimacy, they secretly long for the security of emotional dependence, but are unable to participate in the exchange required of such relationships."

How often have you gone out on first dates and inevitably steel yourself to his initial mandatory monologue? The longer it takes, the more companionable he believes you to be. You have learned to sit there with a fixed smile that you hope looks sympathetic, all the while wondering why he thinks you would be interested in knowing (1) about his manic depression bouts, (2) that his first wife was uninterested in sex, (3) why his last two businesses failed. When he is finished, he asks for the check, tells you what a great time he had and how much you have in common (how could he know since he has not evinced the slightest interest in your life) and when can you meet again.

Women of past generations accepted being emotionally shortchanged in marriage. They viewed such deprivation as a trade-off for support and status. But today's women, like Amy, need neither. Their financial condition is securely in their hands, so fiscal dependency is unnecessary.

IT'S THE MONEY, HONEY

THE AUGUST 3, 2007, front page of the *New York Times* featured a story headed "For Young Earners in Big City, Gap Shifts in Women's Favor." Recent census data show that since 2000, the wage gap between men and women has narrowed, especially in large cities like New York, Los Angeles, Dallas, and a few others. Data showed that "...women of all educational levels from 21 to 30 living in New York City and working full time made 117 percent of men's wages, and even more in Dallas, 120 percent." The experts reasoned that for one thing, "...women have been graduating from college in larger numbers than men, and that many of those women have been gravitating toward major urban areas." They are not marrying right after college, in order to focus on developing the careers for which their education prepared them.

In today's business page, it is not unusual to see women pictured as CEOs of major corporations earning the same obscenely astronomical salaries as men in those positions. Limos, company jets, huge expense accounts—these prestigious perks that used to be For Men Only and were only available to the executive's spouse (if she was lucky enough not to have been jettisoned for a glamorous thirty-year-old Trophy Wife) are heady, exciting stuff women can now earn on their own. The hectic schedule and time demands required in order to reach the top and stay there are often incompatible with a successful home life. Some women may consider this a sacrifice they are not willing to make; others are thrilled with their personal success and find the high-powered life the culmination of their dreams.

Amy said that her mother used to nag her to settle down and marry, "but now she sees how exciting and fulfilling my life is and admits maybe she's a bit envious. She spent her life tied to the house and the needs of my father—he did what he wanted, and she did what he wanted. I do what I want."

AGE IS NO LONGER A FACTOR

WE CAN HEAR readers saying to themselves right about here, "Sure, she's having a great time. She's pretty, only in her thirties, and still attractive to men. But what's going to happen when she hits fifty—who's going to want her, and how great will her life be then?"

Today, age is no longer the gauge of attractiveness or a deterrent to sexual and social activity. Where it would have been regarded as unseemly for an older woman to date (if she was a widow, her children would have been mortified), today's single women of all ages go off on weekends with men friends (and register under their own names, no fake gold bands required) and in fact, have a series of relationships (which used to be called "affairs" and were discussed only in deliriously scandalized whispers, not in front of the children, of course). Life and love go on right up until death does its part. Florida is filled with men and women in their sixties, seventies, and eighties who date, dance, and sleep around. They talk about sex with the same horniness as their grandchildren. In fact, conversations overheard among some sexy seniors sounded remarkably similar to those in any high-school locker room.

Today, maturity is fashionable in both women and men, and age is no longer seen to dim allure. Young men find older women attractive as indeed they are, which has served to increase the supply side of suitors for all women. Single and sixty can now mean rock and roll rather than the rocking chair.

One woman we interviewed proudly claimed, "I feel good about the way I look. It is easy to meet someone I like and am attracted to. They are usually much younger. I'm sixty-three, and they are usually thirty-four to forty-five."

THE DISPARITY BETWEEN their ages may seem extreme, although not if it occurred the other way around with the man being thirty years older. An old guy with a young chick, that's supposed to be. But many of life's "supposed-to-be's" have been cast aside these days thanks to the devout iconoclasm the "Why Generation"—the group of people who came of age in the sixties, who changed our accepted ways of living with one simple word "Why?" It's amazing how easily time-honored traditions and patterns of behavior can be withered by the simple method of questioning their validity.

Years ago, if a forty-two-year-old mother wanted to go back to college, she would have been told the idea was ridiculous and would never have thought to ask "why?" As a result of today's questioning the givens, older women have gone back to school and back into the work force, which has given both those areas a new heterogeneity that seems perfectly natural. For perhaps the first time, young men are working with older women in peer situations and can perceive them as people rather than as mothers or teachers, which was the only context in which they had dealt with them in the past.

Young men are being exposed to the charms and sexual attractiveness of women of all ages and are reacting normally, like falling in love. Unburdened by the man-must-be-older rule in relationships that has been accepted for centuries, they are choosing women solely by desirability rather than age. Like so many time-honored customs, current evaluation and examination in-dicate that it's time to stop honoring it because the cause for its creation is gone.

Why was it always expected that a woman would marry a man older than she? Because historically man was the breadwin-ner and woman the homemaker, and a man did not marry until he was financially secure and able to support a wife and family. Since women were ready for childbearing in their teens and men not established until their twenties and often thirties, she married someone older for security and he married someone younger for fecundity.

Let's not forget that women were, until fairly recently, re-garded as lesser than men in the brain department. In 1859, in his book *The Ordeal of Richard Feverel*, George Meredith wrote, "I expect that Woman will be the last thing civilized by Man." They didn't let us near the ballot box until 1920. What did a mere wom-an know about politics, government, law, finance, business, life? She needed a man to "take care of her." Like Nora in Ibsen's *A Doll's House*, she was to be treated like a child with her life controlled totally by her husband/father. Building on this initial assumption that women are inept idiots who need the strong guidance of male competence, women have always coupled with older men. The difference could be five years or fifteen years; any disparity is con-sidered respectable as long as he has the seniority.

But along came the "Why Generation," who had made all kinds of history by refusing to accept any tradition or convention without a sensible rationale, case by case. We made a war, and the young men refused to attend. We told the young women that it's customary to date older men, and they wanted reasons for the restriction. Today's woman is a lawyer, executive, welder, police-woman, banker, executive, or business owner who is making a solid living and handling the details of her own life capably without the aid of male management. She no longer has to depend on a man for security, so why does he have to be "established," "settled," and older?

Will this seniority ensure a man's greater stability or sense? Of course not. In the first place, wisdom does not come with age, only experience does. If a man is not overly bright at twenty, he is not going to blossom into brilliance at forty. Why assume that older means wiser? And in the second place, even if it did, who needs it? If someone is looking for a sage, superior mate, that someone could just as well be the man as well as the woman. Where is it written that the woman must look up to the man? And that goes literally as well as figuratively. Why should the man always have to be taller? Why is it that when a six-foot male dates a five-foot female, it's acceptable, even adorable. But when a short man and a tall woman fall in love, it is considered comical. If you stop to think about it, isn't this perception just an extension of the conception that big daddy must take care of the little helpless woman and anything else is an aberration?

Today's woman sees no reason to restrict her social relationships by age and feels totally free to explore the attractions of younger as well as older men since she no longer has to depend upon a man for support and security.

And now we come to sexual attractiveness. A woman in her thirties is at her peak of loveliness. In her forties, she has ripened into a mature beauty. At fifty, she can be luscious and in her sixties, have an aura of elegant sensuality.

It has always been perfectly acceptable for a rich, famous man to cavort with young beautiful women. He's attracted to their looks, and they're turned on by his power. With today's open equality of the sexes, flip the roles, and it still works. A rich and famous woman can attract a young handsome man. If both their needs are being met, then it's right.

But it's not only the rich and famous who have reversed the sex roles in May/December relationships, as is indicated by the woman who responded to a column that appeared in the *Miami Herald*.

Commenting on an earlier column about women dating younger men, a woman wrote: "I was seventy last July. My husband of forty years died five years ago. I have a fifty-seven-year-old lover. On Sundays, a sixty-one-year-old man takes me to breakfast and to church services. I have to keep him in his place. My thirty-two-year-old income-tax man approached me for a date and I had to refuse because of his obvious intentions." The columnist responded in print: "You certainly have found a solution to the problem of 'there are no men of my age around.' My guess is that you are communicating a youthfulness and vitality that, along with the maturity of your years, makes for a very attractive combination to many men."

Being single at fifty is no less interesting than being single at thirty. You have the same freedom of choice and activities and can have a wonderful exciting life or a comfortably quiet one according to your own preference.

MARRIAGE? THEN THERE'S NO "ME" ANYMORE

LIL IS A tall, rangy fifty-two-year-old woman whose flowing grey-flecked black hair, large blue un-made-up eyes, defined cheekbones, and uncalculated casual clothes convey an attractiveness that defies the conventional standards of prettiness.

An art major in college, she set off on a varied career that has included establishing her own art gallery, which she eventually sold, acting as curator for a private art collector, running a shop that sold artifacts. At this point in her life, she has become a private consultant to corporate art purchasers and commutes between London and New York, where she lives in an apartment that is cluttered with paintings and sculpture and two Siamese cats who thread their way adroitly through pre-Columbian art pieces and canvasses that are stacked up on the floor against chairs and tables. She paints and continues to sell her paintings, as well as those of other artists.

Lil was married at age thirty-two for three years to a charming man who was twenty years older than she and with whom she had lived for two years. The marriage was something she did not want, but was the result of maternal pressure from, as Lil describes her, "a Victorian Southern belle mother who finally got to me.

"I have never wanted to have children, so why on earth did I get married? After three years together, I found myself bored, restless, and wondering what I was doing there. I couldn't see myself building a future with him, so I left."

"My relationships last three years," she said matter-of-factly. "It has become a pattern in my life. The first two years are romantic and exciting, but then I find I have to put so much energy and time into the relationship that my work begins to suffer. It takes too much out of me, and there's no 'me' anymore. I resent that. Also, I don't like being perceived as a 'couple'—it's a whole different thing, and you lose your individuality. That's how you're seen when you are married. You are lumped together into a take-it-or-leave-it twosome. 'Love her, hate him so let's forget them both'—who wants that? My mother used to insist that I need a man to take care of me. What for? I have an assistant who pays my bills and an accountant who takes care of my income tax."

Lil has had a series of relationships—some of them sexual and some of them platonic.

"I have a wonderful male friend in London now. He's an absolutely delightful escort and friend. We go to theater, visit his friends, go out for dinner. We enjoy each other tremendously. But we have both deliberately avoided sex because that changes the entire configuration of a relationship. I would never think of living with him, either, because it would be disaster. He's a real superfastidious Mr. Tidy, and as you can see from my apartment, I'll never get the *House Beautiful* award.

"In fact, I have never met any man with whom I would want to spend my life. Obviously, it works for some people. There are lots of women who are happily married or have long-term serious intimate relationships. But for me, the thought of spending every day forever with the same person is horrifying. It just would never work for me. There are some dependent kind of women who need to be with someone all the time, who just can't seem to be by themselves. There are actually women who have asked me how to be alone, for God's sakes. I ask them how they can be with someone they don't like. There are men who can't be alone, either. One guy I know buys two tickets night after night for different activities. He's terrified of being alone. It's as though it brands him a social failure. He just cannot face being by himself. But if you met him, you wouldn't want to be with him, either. He's an inane twit with the inner resources of a snail.

"I see no marriage among my friends that I would want. In fact, I see married friends living in intolerable situations. I spent Thanksgiving with a couple—it was a horror. She gave up her career as an editor fifteen years ago because she wanted a family. She married this man who treats her absolutely sadistically. He storms around the house, is always in a fury of some sort over some minor infraction, he's demanding and demeans her constantly. They have a child, poor thing, who's been in therapy for years. With all that yelling and anger, what else could you expect?

"Married people frequently ask me why I don't get married. I respond with 'Why do you stay married when you're so miserable?'"

IN RELATIONSHIPS, MARRIAGE IS FOR BUYERS; I'M A RENTER

WHEN SHE WAS fourteen years old, Vera's father walked into the park one day and shot himself in the head.

He left his family—a wife, Vera, and her younger sister—with a sense of terrible sadness and guilt. ("Why wasn't our love enough for him?") And for Vera a lasting distrust of men and the so-called secure solidity of marriage.

Today, at fifty-seven, Vera is a lovely woman with prematurely white hair that, according to a recent article in the Style section of the *New York Times*, has become a statement of defiance by women today. She has had many careers and leads a life of total independence that she sees no reason to change.

"What can marriage give me that will make my life any better?" She looks at the marriages of friends and family and sees nothing but negatives that by far outweigh any of the promised positives. Like all the women we interviewed who had chosen never to marry, her perceptions leaned toward noting the aggravations and offenses caused by husbands that served to justify her distrust of men and marriage. It's easy to observe fights between spouses that make you glad you're not bound by his demands and go home after a dinner party where the oversoused host tactlessly hurt his wife with comments about her lousy cooking—and be so relieved to return to your pleasant solitude.

Vera made a statement at the beginning of our interview. "I want you to know that I never ever wanted to get married. I've always been terrified of making a mistake. I'm not good at establishing relationships, I'm lousy at retaining them—the only thing I'm good at socially is leaving."

What about familial and social pressure to get married? Didn't her mother and aunts burden her with "so when?" Yes, while she was away at college, her mother would send her clippings of friends' engagements and weddings. And when she came home from a date, her mother would question her about his suitability. When Vera responded that she didn't particularly like the guy, her mother would always say, "You have to give him a chance." Vera's answer was always "Why?" She claims to be a perfectionist and saw no reason to have to groom and train a guy to please her. No one ever could persuade her that her life would be in any way improved by the presence of a husband.

"I have no problem being alone—I'm never lonely. I love to travel and meet and talk to people. I love my total independence. I am accountable to no one, but me. From what I see of marriages, they all require accommodation and compromise that I am not willing to make."

She has had numerous relationships. But only with married men. Of course, they were unavailable, which suited her need to have no possible strings. The last man she was very much in love with, but when his wife found out about her, Vera could not in good conscience continue. "I couldn't stand the idea of hurting another woman. When she didn't know, it was OK. But when he told me his wife learned about us—they had kids, too—I told him it was over."

She has developed her own rules of morality that apply to men. They are not trustworthy, they are not dependable. Her father betrayed them by ignoring the responsibility of marriage and parenthood. Her single life guarantees that she will always be free of the potential pain and disappointment imposed on women by weak and selfish men.

Vera was drawn to having affairs with married men because in doing so, she was only confirming her lack of respect for all men. In her view, their willingness to break nuptial vows only proved how untrustworthy, weak, and immoral they were.

She pointed out that she had never seen any happy marriages in her own family. Her aunt had married twice, both marriages ending badly. Her sister married a man twenty-five years her senior and was still together with him although Vera could not understand why. She related all the negatives her sister was accepting and could not see any possible reason to stay with this man. But as we pointed out, various life elements have various rates of importance to people. Her sister apparently felt that coming home every night to a man who had cooked dinner (he was retired and elderly) or took her out to nice restaurants (he was wealthy) was better than coming home to a solitary microwave chicken pie in front of TV, and since his increasing number of geriatric ailments were being handled by his excellent health-care provisions and his grown children from a previous marriage, her responsibilities were minimal, she had someone to talk to, and all in all, the trade-off worked for her.

All of Vera's relatives had multiple marriages with much unpleasantness involved. Eight cousins had produced only a total of two kids among them. She herself loved children—her career involved working with them—but she never wanted to have any. After speaking for more than two hours, she casually mentioned that she had an abortion when she was twenty-two, and of all the decisions she had made in her life, this was one she never for a second regretted.

In high school and college, her social life was not exactly glittering. "I was never good at that boy/girl stuff. If I liked a boy, I didn't know how to let him know it, and if a boy liked me, I never seemed to know what to do next like other girls did. I was always uncomfortable around boys. And men. I'm not good at intimacy."

When she spoke of the various men she has been with, the only one whom she still talks to and of whom she says "I would have married had he asked" is gay, something they hadn't realized early on. But perhaps the air of unavailability was what attracted her in the first place, although they were too young to be aware of his gender preference at the time.

Vera's sense of self is very strong and her honesty and morality are obviously deeply ingrained. Sometimes in interviews, a subject comes across as posturing, with firm statements that she would like to persuade you, as well as herself, are real. Vera did not try to take any position or offer any proof of her sincerity. "This is me, this is what I believe in, and this is how I choose to live." Nor did she, as many people do, mock the decisions of people who do not subscribe to her beliefs.

From all these statements, you would expect a hard, tough lady, but Vera is a soft-spoken, gentle person who has built a new and satisfying career teaching young children to become aware of the world and the differences in people who inhabit it.

"I've often heard people say one must work at a marriage to make a go of it," she said. "If I was given the choice of working at a marriage or working at my career in order to make a success, I'd pick the career."

For what is wedlock forced, but a hell, An age of discord and continual strife? Whereas the contrary bringest bliss and is a pattern of celestial peace.
　　　　　　—WILLIAM SHAKESPEARE, KING HENRY VI

5

NO WAY WEDLOCK

IT'S HARD TO imagine in these days of violent films filled with blatant sex scenes that in the fifties, people flocked to see a movie where Debbie Reynolds tried to get Frank Sinatra to marry her and move to Scarsdale in a movie called *The Tender Trap*. The actress Doris Day was famous for being forever virginally unapproachable until matrimony was ensured. Marriage was the goal of the leading ladies in movies of the 1940s and 1950s, and it was a universal assumption that connubial bliss was craved by females and evaded by men. The inevitable ending to every made-in-Hollywood courtship was that she snared him and they lived happily ever after.

Times have changed. Hollywood has changed. They no longer make "movies," mere frivolous forms of mass entertainment; we now get "films" designed to contribute to their concept of the human condition. Current films and TV depict women who dump men because they need "space." In fact, that word is being used as a dramatic device so frequently that it gives new meaning to the term "space age." Women are as likely to be the deserters as the desertees, and cohabitation rather than commitment is often her choice.

Does art mirror life, or does life mirror art? In a free society such as ours, it happens in a simultaneous explosion. Judging from what we see and hear in both the real world and the world of TV and movies, it is an inescapable fact that today not all women long to marry. And for a variety of reasons, many women actively avoid matrimony and regard that lifestyle as antithetical to happiness.

We now recognize that there are alternatives to marriage. Marriage is no longer regarded as the only way to live, but merely as one of the possible lifestyles one may choose to adopt.

According to the Rutgers "State of Our Union 2007" report quoted earlier, between the early to mid-1990s, the marriage rate in the United States dropped 24 percent; at the same time, the unmarried cohabitation percentage jumped 49 percent.

Marriage creates male/female role assignments that can destroy relationships rather than cement them. Women who feel that they cannot or will not conform to the confines of this dictum may now opt to skip the whole construct and live with a man and derive all the pleasures of conjugality with none of the restrictions.

"JEFF WOULD GET MARRIED TOMORROW.
BUT NOT ME."

JOANNE AND JEFF had been living together for five years and are solidly set into a happy, loving joint existence that combines the conventional components of connubial togetherness with the romantic aura of courtship.

The house they had just bought showed signs of the extensive do-it-yourself renovation that they were doing together. There was a casual, inviting warmth to the décor, and Joanne projected the secure contentment of a woman who knew what she wanted and was fortunate enough to have it. The scene was perfect. The only items missing were the picket fence—and the marriage license.

"Marriage is just a piece of paper that could have a negative impact. This relationship is the best thing that's ever happened to me, and no way am I going to rock the boat. Everything is wonderful as is—why do something that might change it?"

JOANNE IS AN attractive, vivacious thirty-eight-year-old woman who had been married at nineteen and divorced at twenty-one. "It wasn't anyone's fault. When I got married, I expected to live happily ever after. Like magic. After a while, I realized something was very wrong, only I didn't know what. I had this crazy, unreal image of a wife and a husband, and I was angry and upset all the time because neither of us could fill our roles. He couldn't manage what I thought men were supposed to handle in a marriage, and I didn't want to be the kind of person I thought a wife had to be. It was really dumb. But all I could see was me becoming one of those women like my mother who can't drive, and I went nuts."

Hers was the classic case of a marriage that failed because of the commonest of reasons: unrealistic expectations. Joanne is naturally aggressive and independent, but she believed that implicit in "I do" was that she not do and that overnight, the marriage ceremony would change her into a submissive Suzy Homemaker and her husband into a strong take-charge guy. When she realized she detested being a helpless female and resented that her new husband (who was all of twenty) didn't instantly know how to balance a checkbook and handle family finances, she felt trapped and furious. It was untenable, and they divorced.

Thenceforth, Joanne regarded marriage as the worst form of bondage. She saw it as a destructive force that changed lives and altered psyches and personalities. In a sense, she was right. The old adage that you don't know someone until you live with him or her is true, except that often the someone you don't know is you.

There is no way you can anticipate how you will react to living with another person until you do it. There is give-and-take in every relationship, but how do you know how much you can give or take until you are there? It is easy to assume you know yourself and your levels of tolerance toward specific behaviors. But what you cannot predict is your willingness to lower those thresholds of acceptance in response to signs of love and kindness that bring you joy and happiness. You cannot stand boorishness, and it drives you nuts when your guy tells tasteless jokes that indicate to you an important lack of sophistication and sensitivity. You grind your teeth and swear that the next time he does it, you're out of there. But on your birthday, he surprised you by bringing a cake to your office, and when you were sick, he insisted on staying home from work in order to take care of you. How can you not love living with a guy like that? It's a trade-off...like everything else in life.

MARRIAGE CAN CREATE UNREALISTIC EXPECTATIONS

"I LOVE OUR life together," continued Joanne. "I can't see where marriage could add anything positive, but I have seen where it could be a big negative. Getting married almost destroyed my friend's relationship. She had been living with her friend for eight years. They were great together until they decided they wanted kids, so they got married.

"The minute they became husband and wife, everything went haywire. She expected some kind of magic transformation...like he would suddenly act like a Husband, whatever that meant. For instance, she was furious because he couldn't rewire the kitchen.

A husband is supposed to do handyman things, right? That's what her dad did, so of course, all husbands should. For gosh sakes, the guy had trouble screwing in a light bulb, and now she expects him to be Mr. Goodwrench? Here they had been going along happy as clams, enjoying life, and then this big ceremony takes place, and everything changes because she figures they have to get serious now and make a Life Plan, set up a budget, buckle down to the business of living, and she becomes a major nag.

"They nearly broke up, but a little therapy helped straighten things out, and they made it OK. But who needs that? Jeff and I are happy just the way we are, and to my mind, there's absolutely no benefit in going through some legal stuff. What for? I've seen it too many times, when they get the piece of paper, expectations change, and suddenly everything's supposed to be perfect. Things they used to do or not do, or used to let slide, are not acceptable anymore. Jeff and I, we just take life as it comes, and we're happy."

Joanne had met Jeff in her office. She was a manager with the telephone company where he worked as a technician.

"He's shy," she said with a laugh. "I had to ask him out. Twice! We dated, and then it began to develop into something good. After a year, it had passed the infatuation stage and grown into love. Then I lost the lease on my apartment and had to find a place to live. It just seemed natural for me to move in with Jeff."

Buying the house was also a practical decision. At income-tax time, their accountant pointed out how much money they were sending down the tax tubes by not having the benefits of deductions like mortgage interest. They had minor difficulty in getting a joint mortgage since they were not married. "The bank asked us for a 'statement of relationship,' which I thought was nonsense. If we bought the property together as an investment, no one would question it. But since we intended to live there, that somehow changed things. We put ourselves down as 'spousal equivalents,' " she said with a big laugh, "and they accepted it." Now they delight in owning their own home and, at the slow casual pace that suits them both, are renovating the place a bit at a time. The house has three bedrooms—their room, a den, and a guest room. No nursery, and none anticipated.

"We don't want children," she said emphatically. "We decided that early on and haven't changed our minds. In fact, we're so definite, that this year Jeff had a vasectomy."

For two years after her divorce, Joanne had worked in a facility for abused and neglected children. She spent her days with children of all ages and often had the satisfaction of helping to turn around the life of an almost doomed child.

ALTHOUGH SHE LIKES children, she realized that she does not have the patience for the responsibility of a day-to-day relationship and does not have the desire or talent for parenting.

"I have twenty-one nieces and nephews, and I dearly love them all. We have great times together, they know I'm for fun and their mothers are for serious. I really enjoy spending the day with one or two at a time, and I can be patient and totally free with them because I know that in a couple of hours, I can go home to peace and quiet and relax. I make a marvelous aunt, but I'd make a lousy mother."

Joanne grew up in an Irish-Catholic family of ten children. "If you haven't shared a four-bedroom, one-bathroom house with twelve people, you can't understand the pleasures of privacy and the joys of living with just one person.

"My parents had some marriage! We never heard raised voices in our house because they never spoke to each other except about household and family things. My father worked two jobs, so he wasn't around all that much, and when he was home, he was tired. I never heard them exchange a word about their feelings. I never saw them kiss each other. Their only relationship was in producing ten babies. We have friends today with that kind of marriage. If it weren't for their kids, there wouldn't be anything between them at all."

PARENTAL ACCEPTANCE

COMING FROM A strongly religious home as she did, Joanne anticipated some remonstration and shock from her parents when she and Jeff moved in together.

"I was the first of my friends to divorce. You have to know that in our house the word 'divorce' was like the 'F' curse word. So I figured my mom and dad would be horrified because I was 'living in sin.' But not at all. They see how happy Jeff and I are and how we live a quiet life. We don't have wild parties or hang out in bars. My father's only comment was, 'I guess it's OK as long as you're happy.' And my mother's reaction when I told her I did not intend to marry or have children was simply, 'If that's how God meant for you to be, then it's right.' That was the closest I've felt to my mother in my whole life, and I'm grateful we had that chance to finally touch each other. She died last year."

THE FREEDOM OF NONMARRIAGE

ALTHOUGH JOANNE AND Jeff display a commitment to a shared future, there is an undercurrent of independence in her demeanor that adds to rather than subtracts from her obvious sense of security. She has learned that being alone is taking responsibility for oneself as everyone must ultimately do in order to survive. Trust and interdependability are integral parts of any good relationship, but dependence leads to subordination and the eventual diminishing of self.

"I admit I like keeping my eye on the exit door. And I like not having to be beholden to anyone. Like when I got this great job offer that meant leaving the telephone company where Jeff and I work. Now no one leaves the telephone company, a job there is for life. But this sounded so exciting and such a terrific opportunity, and besides, I like the stimulation of change. I wanted to talk it over with Jeff, but he was away on a hunting trip that week. So I made the decision myself and took the job, and I love it. If we were married, I'd have to discuss it with my husband. Not being married makes me feel that I have more control over my own life. And that's what I must have."

THE RESTRICTIONS OF MARRIAGE

"LOVE IS CONSIDERATION, and marriage is obligation. When that certificate comes, the whole feeling changes."

This came from twenty-five-year-old Melissa, who has lived with the man she loves for more than two years and has finally gotten him to understand that her refusal to marry is not a rejection of him, but an important affirmation of self for her.

Melissa comes from a small town in the Midwest and went east to college. She met Paul through friends, and they fell in love quickly. But her schedule and his job resulted in their seeing each other on weekends only. "We had dates, like Bobby and Margie going to the movies." After they talked and talked and learned about each other's background, childhood, feelings about life and issues, and sated the tremendous hunger to know all about the one you love from the moment of birth, they realized they wanted more than just the dating relationship.

"I heard him telling our friends about occurrences of the day that I hadn't heard before. And we knew we wanted to live together, to see each other at breakfast, and to know we would see each other every night. So I moved into his apartment."

Their parents were puzzled. If you love each other, why not marry? But Melissa had associations with the word "marriage" that she knew would destroy their relationship. So they have been living together happily and intend to do so indefinitely.

"Marriage would change me, I know it," she says. "I can't bear the thought of being cast into a mold. I would feel restricted, typecast, and I'd hate it. Right now, I do all the 'female' things in the house—the cooking, shopping, and cleaning. I do it because if I didn't, the place would be a pigsty, and we'd eat fast food every night. Paul is a slob, and he just doesn't care. But if we married, somehow I would resent being pushed into that role because it's expected, demanded. To me it would be a tyranny I couldn't endure."

MELISSA HAS WORKED hard on herself to become self-sufficient and independent, and she sees marriage as a threat to all she has accomplished. "I love Paul, and right now I want to spend the rest of my life with him. But I know that I'm a better person because we're not married. I wouldn't like me, he wouldn't like me, and it would all end up in disaster."

Melissa is burdened with the image of her mother and grandmother and all the women she knew who lived conventional homemaker lives and never questioned their roles. Women were the ones who had the responsibility of making the marriage work with little input or emotional support from their husbands.

She had a father who was never "there for us" and a mother who accepted the deprivation as women historically have done. She saw the marital male hierarchy of the dominant father and the subordinate wife, and the injustices imposed, and she feared that being married would make her view herself as one of those pathetic subservient wretches and would destroy her love for Paul and his for her.

"I meet women who think marriage gives them stability and reliability. I see it as doing just the opposite to me. It would make me shaky because I would lose confidence in myself and my own ability to make decisions."

Melissa is keenly aware of the difficulty women go through in order to attain parity with men. A great part of the travail is the personal struggle to build belief in your own strength and power before you can expect to be viewed as equal. She had fought that battle and saw marriage as a threat to her hard-won strength and self-sufficiency.

"Right now, Paul wants us to do everything as a couple. He has a much greater need than I to be together. I want us to have three lives—his, mine, and ours—but he wants one only. When I'm stuck at work, I call, and he gives me a hard time because he hates when I'm late. I love him and don't like to make him unhappy, but if I was married, I would feel more obligated to be home on time. Now I feel freer to do what is right for me. If I got a wonderful job offer in another part of the country or wanted to relocate to a different climate, we would talk it over. I can't see ever wanting to leave Paul because I love him so much. But if he just balked arbitrarily and I felt strongly that I had to go, I would feel free to do so. I couldn't do that if we were married. I can't envision that happening, but I need to know that I could. I'm here with Paul because I want to be, not because I have to be."

YOU CAN'T RITE THE WRONGS

"LOTS OF OUR friends got married and divorced— even before they paid off their Visa card expenses for the wedding. I don't know what miracle they expected to happen when they got married, but obviously it didn't."

Relationships are built on love and trust, not ritual. Many of Melissa's friends thought that marriage would cement relationships and convert what were merely preliminary facades into permanent installations. It doesn't work that way. If there isn't enough there to hold things together before marriage, going through a rite will not correct the wrong. Instead of giving their feelings for each other a chance to develop, they regarded marriage as an acceleration device: "Once we're husband and wife, we'll have the sense of commitment to make it work." Then they go through all the months of festive buildup planning for the wedding, consuming brides' magazines, buying the gown, selecting bridesmaids, silver patterns, invitations, and get carried away with the magic-moment concept that says they will get married and live happily ever after.

Finally the big event takes place. All the frenzied months of planning are consummated, it's all over, and suddenly they are no longer basking in the golden glow of being the special fussed-over bride-and-groom center of attention ("What a beautiful bride she made!" "Wasn't it a gorgeous wedding?"). Now they are alone together, nothing special, just another married couple...and then comes the letdown.

To their shock, the experience, no matter how costly, enchanting, and glorious, hasn't changed either one an iota. If there were things about each other that bothered them before, being married did not erase them. Marriage is not a rite of purification.

In fact, if anything, you are even more annoyed because you are now dealing with disappointment over your unrealistic expectation that the ceremony would be a cure-all. You're angry because things did not become perfect instantly and being married did not make either of you different people than you were before. So marriage becomes the problem, not the solution.

IT'S EASIER TO NOT GET MARRIED

ROSE, A VIVACIOUS woman who just turned thirty-nine, and Joe, a handsome, athletic-looking man of forty-four, have been living together for more than ten years, and she never once entertained the idea of getting married.

"What for?" says Rose. "Getting married is an active step. It involves going out and doing something for what seems to me to be no real reason at all. We're together, we're a team, we love each other, what will the piece of paper do for us that we don't already have?"

Rose works in the computer industry, as does Joe. Recently, they decided to join forces and started a business together. "So we already have a legal tie—we're incorporated," said Rose.

Ten years ago, they started out with a purely sexual relationship that grew into something much more. Each had lived through many lifestyle changes, and this seemed to be, at first, merely another casual encounter. They soon perceived that they wanted to be with each other all the time and finally moved in together. Over the years, they had their fights, ups and downs, and identity crises.

"I'm much more confident now than I used to be," says Rose. "I'm more demanding because I have a pride in myself that took years to build. Joe helped me, but it's made his life with me a little tougher. He sometimes feels somewhat threatened, but he wants us to stay together so he's changed, too. If you were to ask who gives more, who compromises more, I'd say that for the first five years, I gave 70 percent and he 30 percent. During the last five years, the figures have flipped. But I've never said I'd leave because the one good thing I got from my mother was that you have to stick with it."

Like most women's, Rose's reaction to marriage was colored by her perception of her parents' relationship. Her mother was an immigrant who married an American Southerner whose business took him away from home a great deal. An only child, Rose—as well as her mother—was alone much of the time, and her mother's resentment and sense of abandonment were a constant source of discussion. Rose grew up with a jaundiced view of the institution of marriage and for years, could not understand her mother's prodding Rose to get married when she herself was so obviously unhappy with the results.

"The whole thought of marriage is scary," says Rose. "I do not want to live like my mother and father did. There's an eternity aspect to the whole thing that I don't like. Sure, I'd like to have someone next to me in twenty years, but marriage doesn't guarantee that." Neither Joe nor Rose wants children. They feel that there are plenty of people out there reproducing and keeping mankind going. If they want to make an impact on the next generation, there are lots of ways to work with children to pass along their knowledge.

IN EVERY ASPECT of their life, they live like a married couple. Joe cooks because he's better at it. They worry about each other and feel responsible to each other. In fact, during the interview I had with Rose, she looked at her watch constantly and then excused herself to call Joe to say she would be late and he should have dinner without her. When I pointed this out to her, she said, "Of course we're considerate of each other because we care for each other. That's love, not necessarily marriage. Marriage is purely a social tradition that has no impact on the reality of living with someone. It's supposed to give permanence, but I assure you that if either one of us was unhappy and wanted out, that piece of paper wouldn't hold us."

FLEXIBILITY, FREEDOM, AND ROMANCE, TOO

THERE IS AN aura to unwedded bliss that was apparent in each woman interviewed, a sense of certainty about themselves, a pride and happiness that come from feeling loved, secure, and excited with life. Although none of them voiced it, they are subconsciously proud of themselves for breaking the rules and winning.

Granted that it's easier today than ever before to live together without benefit of clergy, you are still fighting the battle of convention and parental pressure. The way society is set up, it is passive to get married and active to avoid it. Yet these women have had the courage to decide what is right for them regardless of tradition and the behavior of others. None of them is a radical or in any way different in appearance or action than her peers. They are just ordinary folks, but remember it's just "ordinary folks" who have historically proven to be the catalysts of change. Like the little boy in "The Emperor's New Clothes" who was unafraid to point out that the emperor was naked, these women have pointed out that marriage ain't what it's been cracked up to be and should no longer be regarded as a given.

Another important quality that was palpably obvious in every home visited that is not always present in married households was Romance. Besides the love, caring, and other elements that also exist in successful marriages, there is the romantic excitement generated from his and her knowledge that she is there with him only because she wants to be and not because of the bonds of law or children or convention…that she is free and flexible and as ready as men have always been to take off should he fail her or the relationship become unfulfilling.

When Cynthia was on a TV daytime talk show some years ago, she brought up this "air of romance in unmarried households" that doesn't seem to exist in conventionally married homes—and the audience erupted in indignation. It was filled with middle-aged married ladies who obviously felt their way of life was being criticized; one jumped up and shouted, "I can always bring romance into my home—I just put on my sexy black nightgown and peignoir!" When the audience cried out "Right, right!" Cynthia said "Really? Why doesn't he put on a black jockstrap? Why should it always be our responsibility?" The hostess of the show cracked up, but the audience didn't smile.

I never found the companion that was so companionable as solitude. We are for the most part more lonely when we go abroad among men than when we stay in our chambers. A man thinking or working is always alone, let him be where he will.
—Henry David Thoreau

6

ALONE IS NOT LONELY

CYNTHIA LIVES ALONE and is frequently asked if she is lonely. She is puzzled by the assumption that the presence of another person in the house precludes loneliness. She is especially bemused when the question is posed by a couple who haven't spoken a civil word to each other in years except maybe "Pass the salt."

A very wise and lovely elderly woman was asked after her husband of fifty years died whether she might not be lonely. She answered with a sad smile, "Sometimes you can be lonelier living with someone than living alone."

According to the *American Heritage Dictionary of the English Language*, the definition of loneliness is "Dejected by the awareness of being alone." Thus it is a condition that is not a fact, but merely a personal reaction to the situation of singleness. It's not the presence of people that prevents loneliness; it's the presence of a sense of self-adequacy.

Being by yourself can be a liberation from those conscious or subconscious pulls that force you to cater to the needs of others.

If your self-importance has been built on how well you respond to the demands of people around you, then you have never given yourself a chance to understand what really makes you happy. Being alone affords you the luxury of learning about you.

Widows who have spent a lifetime busily taking care of their families and have rarely spent a moment alone profess to be lonely at first until they learn the lovely self-indulgence of doing what they want and building their lives around their needs and not someone else's.

THE LUXURY OF BEING ALONE

A DIVORCED WOMAN whose daughter went off to college reported that instead of the lonely empty-nest depression everyone predicted, she experienced a soaring sense of glorious freedom.

"I don't have to listen to blasting music anymore. I don't have to keep screaming to get off her cell phone and do her homework. I'm free."

Being alone can be a wonderful soul-nurturing state—if you enjoy your own company. There is tremendous pleasure in giving yourself the luxury of time to mull and muse about your feelings and reactions to the day's activities—in peaceful solitude. And to do just what you want without worrying about others' opinions.

A woman who had a live-in relationship took a long-distance phone call from her partner. "You'll be home tonight?" Her face fell. "I thought you were coming home next week. OK—see you." She hung up and said, "Nuts. I was so looking forward to a week alone." And went on to explain that living together was not always easy.

"It's just that he has an opinion on everything— and lets me know. Even when I schedule a manicure, he'll say 'Again? You just had one.' I love him, but I wish he'd keep out of my life a little."

There are evenings when you may want to burst into the house and share the day's happenings with someone who cares such as when you were a child and dashed home to tell your mother about the A in History. But there are those many evenings when you fall in exhausted and long to just unwind quietly. After you've cooled down, had your drink and dinner, and feel like talking, that's when you get on the phone and chat with friends to your heart's content, without annoying interruptions demanding how much longer you intend to blab and snide allusions to the motormouth propensities of women.

EATING ALONE AND LOVING IT

ONE OF THE most frequent questions we live-alones get from people who are curious about coping with single living is the "Eating Alone" issue, which is a Rorschach test for positive versus negative self-image.

"You don't cook for yourself, do you...just one person? I guess you eat a sandwich or something over the sink or get those frozen prepared things." Once, Cynthia tried one of those so-called gourmet microwave dinners, and after the second bite which only confirmed the first, she thought the best thing about this meal was that she didn't have to claim her luggage afterward.

Why not cook for yourself? Don't you count? Are you only worthy of a decent meal if you eat in consort?

Eating alone can be one of life's most satisfying epicurean experiences. Like all working people, you are tired at the end of the day, and it can be extremely relaxing to set up a glass of wine on the kitchen counter, turn on the radio, and begin the pleasant, but mindless, preparation of a fine meal. Picture this for a moment: brown rice with onions, mushrooms, walnuts, and sultanas is cooking on the stove, and a cheese-and-zucchini casserole is in the oven while the scallops, garlic, and parsley wait in the fridge for last-minute sautéing. The table in the dining room is set with a placemat and book, and when your dinner is ready, you can let the phone go to voicemail and sit down to savor the flavors of the food.

This doesn't make you an unsocialized misanthrope, but just a person who luxuriates in the rewards of solitude, as well as the conviviality of dining with company. Be happy with yourself, and although you love dinner parties and dining with friends, you can also enjoy eating alone without the cacophony of conversation that often serves to detract from rather than deepen the sensuous satisfaction that can be derived from fine fare.

Many women say they can't bear eating alone. It used to be a common sight to see men at tables for one; now there are just as many women dining in solitary splendor.

One woman said, "If I were alone in a hotel, I'd never go down to the dining room. I'd have them send up room service."

A good part of her reaction, along with that of those who will not dine alone, comes not from fear of aloneness but rather of reluctance to be publicly viewed as unwanted, the old double standard whereby he is alone by choice and she by rejection. That, of course, is nonsense. As is the old bromide that a lone woman is scorned by the maitre d' and relegated automatically to a seat next to the kitchen. Cynthia has been traveling alone and eating alone for years, and the only time she ever ran into restaurant discrimination was in a hotel dining room in Columbus, Ohio. Cynthia waited behind a single man who was asked by the hostess if he wished to be seated at the "travelers' table," which was a large banquet-looking setup filled with men, "and you get a free drink on the house, too," she added with a smile. When Cynthia's turn came, she said, "One?" and started to lead me to a table. "Wait a moment," Cynthia said, "Don't I get offered the free drink and the 'travelers' table'?" "Oh no," the hostess answered immediately, "that's for men only." Cynthia looked at her and said evenly, "Really? That's illegal. Sex discrimination is against the law." The hostess became upset, and her face turned beet red. It had apparently never dawned on her or the management that a policy innovated to make life pleasanter for the traveling man could also apply to the traveling woman. She apologized and after Cynthia assured her that she had no wish to be seated with a bunch of strangers, but would not refuse a free drink, Cynthia was put at a lovely quiet banquette and brought a Bloody Mary and a bottle of wine on the house.

There are many people who shrink at the idea of being alone or doing things alone simply because they have never tried it and fear they will suffer from that nebulous undefined condition of "loneliness." It's not scary to be by yourself. It's wonderful. Loneliness is not a state of being. It's just a state of mind.

"Children begin by loving their parents; as they grow older, they judge them; sometimes they forgive them."
—OSCAR WILDE

7

PARENT POWER

IF YOU RAISE your child to be an independent thinker, when she grows up and kicks all your values and beliefs, have you succeeded or failed?

Parenting is a tricky business. From birth, most kids want to please their parents (except when they reach the Terrible Twos and their teens and seem to want only to torture them). That strong desire for parental approval persists and has become the butt of jokes forever, especially in Jewish families where guilt in trying to please parents is an art form. As in the one about the son who calls home to tell his mother he is planning to marry a non-Jewish girl. "I have to hang up now," says the mother.

"Why?" asks the son.

"Because I have to go and put my head in the oven."

Seeking to please your parents is OK as long as you do not let it cripple you. Their motivation for trying to control your life is usually given as "We only want what's best for you." The real meaning is "We only want you to do what we think is best for you." Frequently, when a mother tries to give her daughter advice on how to handle a specific problem, the daughter answers "Mom, I'm not you." And she's right. How the mother deals with situations is based on her personality, her experience, and her comfort level of behavior. She should not impose it on her daughter.

Your parents have a point of view based on the mores, customs, and beliefs of their lifetime. There have been drastic changes in the past twenty years of what is societally acceptable. Religious intermarriage has become commonplace, interracial marriage has become commonplace, same-sex coupling has become commonplace. If your parents, or in some cases grandparents, find it hard to accept that your life choices are drastically different from theirs—that's their problem.

Michael R. Cunningham, a psychologist who teaches in the communications department at the University of Louisville, conducted a survey of college women to see if, upon graduation, they would prefer to settle down with a high-school teacher who has short workdays, summers off, and spare energy to help raise children, or with a surgeon who earns eight times as much, but works brutal hours; three-quarters of the women said they would choose the teacher. Can you imagine their mothers' opinion of that choice that would deprive them of the chance to boast about their "son-in-law the doctor"?

You cannot base your choice of husband on anyone's feelings but yours, no matter what guilt trips are being imposed upon you by interfering family. We met one young woman suffering from the harassment of her grandparents who are trying to stop her from marrying the man she loves because he is not of their religion. Since she is the eldest of their many grandchildren, the guilt they are trying to lay on her is that she is the family role model who could lead other grandchildren to follow her suit, marry out of the faith and thus destroy the family which has clung to their religion for generations.

No one has the right to block your happiness based on his or her beliefs—religious or cultural. Years ago, and currently in India and other countries, marriages were arranged by parents who paired their children with people they believed would give their children—and them—the greatest possible advantages—not necessarily happiness.

If you meet the man you see yourself spending your life with—go for it. It is up to you and you alone. It may or may not end up a mistake—there are no guarantees in life—but it will be your mistake. Remember, what we are saying is women should never marry for the wrong reasons, and therefore you should examine your motivations before you leap!

PERVERSE PARENTAL PRESSURE

VALERIE GREW UP in what seemed like ideal circumstances— all the comforts of an upper-middle-class family, an only child who had everything a child could want. Well, almost. The home was filled with love: Dad loved mom, and mom was deeply devoted to dad. Valerie was next in line.

Valerie's mother had fallen in love with and married her boss, who was twenty years her senior. Her mother adored her father, and the entire household revolved around his opinions and his needs. Children are extremely sensitive to their parents' true feelings, and Valerie early on realized her role was to submit to their decisions, which rarely considered her desires. They sent her to camp for the summer, and while many parents took that opportunity to travel while the kids were being taken care of and away, Valerie's dad declared Europe was too tourist-packed during the summer; they preferred to vacation in the fall after Valerie returned home, and they left her in the care of a maid. She would come home just as they were going out the door.

Valerie spent her life trying to please them, to get the same level of love they showed for each other. Her total compliance made her parents the envy of all their friends whose children were giving them the usual aggravation of teenage rebellion while Valerie just smiled and followed orders.

VALERIE'S FATHER HAD rather old-fashioned ideas of the importance of "doing the right thing," which meant going to the "right places," wearing the "right clothes," dining in the "right restaurants." To him, and of course his wife, success depended upon fitting in and never making waves. He was delighted with his daughter's submissiveness and boasted that she was "totally average" and thus would always get along well in the world. When it came time to apply for colleges, he told her she must go only to a school in a major city since that would give her the greatest opportunity to meet the man she would marry, college being the time most women acquire husbands. Obedient as always, she attended a university in a metropolitan area and sure enough, upon graduation, became engaged to a young man in her school. She was twenty-one, exactly the right age, too.

Her parents were delighted—he fit the bill to a "t": He was of average intelligence, average appearance, planning to become an average lawyer. He even began to call them "mom" and "dad" when he visited, the conventional son-in-law-to-be. To them, Valerie's future was assured. She now had someone to take care of her for a life that was certain to be a replica of theirs.

The wedding was predictable: tulle-dressed bridesmaids, lots of lovely flowers and good wines. Valerie's parents sighed with pride and relief: Their daughter had followed their guidance and was assured a solid future.

After six months of living in a small apartment in the city near the law school he attended while she taught elementary school and kept house like her mother, Valerie met a new type of friends. Soon, she started to take guitar lessons, yoga lessons, became a vegetarian, and was often not home when her husband arrived expecting dinner on the table. Within three more months, to her parents' shock, she announced she was getting a divorce. No amount of explanation reached them—her rebellion was beyond their understanding.

SHE RETURNED TO her home city, got an apartment, and began dating all sorts of men, all of whom seemed totally unsuitable to her parents. They were horrified at what they saw as promiscuity. They kept hoping she would come to her senses and finally settle down with the "right sort" of man. As the years went on and she had not remarried, her parents were both puzzled and unhappy. When she passed thirty-five, they felt that was it. Who would want to marry an older woman?

When she was thirty-seven, she told them she had met someone who was important to her, and she wanted them to meet him. When she brought Mike home, they were speechless. In the first place, he did not "look good," their first criterion for acceptability. He was the product of a working-class family and uneducated parents. His teeth were crooked, often the result of poor childhood care by parents who could not afford dental work. His sense of style was as far away from Brooks Brothers as you could get, and to top it off, he wore a diamond-stud earring. He had not attended the "right schools," but was a strong, self-made guy who had made a successful life against all odds. Valerie was obviously deeply in love, and she announced they were now living together and would be married within two months.

The wedding was the diametric opposite of her first wedding. No fancy facility, it was held in an American Legion Hall in a small nearby town; no bustling waiters, it was line-up Army style to get your food. Valerie was obviously radiantly happy and barely noticed that her parents had not invited any of their friends to witness what they saw as their shame. The event was attended by dozens of lively, intelligent people the parents had never met, but all of whom were close friends of the wedding couple. Valerie had obviously developed a whole circle of friends whom she had never introduced to them.

VALERIE AND MIKE have been happily married for twenty years. It would be hard not to view Valerie's motivations for marriage as reactive to her parents. She married the first time to please her parents, but it took getting away from them before she felt the freedom to rebel against the deprivations of her childhood and to become herself and not their clone. She married the second time to please herself. The overt simplicity of her second wedding could have been a calculated punitive measure to prove to her parents that she had kicked their foolish bourgeois values. Better yet, it showed that she no longer cared about their approval and was happy just being herself.

The second time was right because she followed her own instincts, developed through years of independence as a single woman.

THE DOCTOR'S WIFE

MARCIA WAS A bright, awkward, and untidy girl who was class president in high school, liked by girls, and admired but never adored by boys. She grew up in a community that was renowned for its affluence but was actually a mix of modest to millionaire homes where socializing was based on interest rather than income, and class distinctions were blurred. Marcia's academician parents' unconcern for aesthetics and luxuries was obvious from the slapdash look of their home, which was furnished in early Salvation Army.

Her mother was an extremely unattractive woman who seemed to feel that having snared a handsome husband relieved her of the necessity of even attempting to look appealing. Like many children who are brought up in a household where money and its attendant pleasures are unimportant, Marcia and her younger brother craved riches. "I'm going to be a doctor and make lots of money," she announced and applied to the top-level colleges that would route her to medical-school acceptance. It did not go easily for Marcia, nothing did, and she was turned down by all but one good school, where the last-minute wait listing paid off, and she was accepted.

She worked hard because she knew that high marks were mandatory if one sought admission to crowded U.S. medical schools. College was demanding, but she was determined—and lonely. Then she met Glenn in one of her classes and for the first time, found a man who thought her attractive. She fell madly in love. What she did not know was that Glenn found all women attractive and had a lusty sex drive that took him from one bed to the other with promiscuous regularity. She saw him whenever he wished and slept with him at will—his. She was totally infatuated and virtually enslaved, and her schoolwork suffered, and for the first time, her grades slipped below the As and Bs required for med-school admission.

Then came the worst blow of all. She got herpes, an incurable venereal infection that she knew had to have come from Glenn since he was the first and only man with whom she had sex. She confronted him with her anger, and he deflected it casually by seducing her again. The destructive relationship persisted all through college although she tried to break it up from time to time. But like all obsessed victims of unrequited passions, she could never resist Glenn's demands.

By the time she was graduated, Marcia had managed to pull up her grade-point average, but demoralized by Glenn's behavior, her M-CAT medical-school-qualifying exam performance was lackluster. She knew she could do far better and decided to take the exam again the next year, when she felt that a stronger M-CAT score further enhanced by working laboratory experience could improve her candidacy. To that end, she took a job as a biologist in a hospital. There she met the second man in her life, Richard, a medical student.

Like her father, Richard was handsome and taciturn. Marcia was intelligent and sociable and enjoyed stimulating conversation, but recognized that men did not have the same talent as women for chitchat and small talk. Richard was unable to show affection other than sexually but seemed to have an attachment to her that she found gratifying. However, his long silences and unwillingness or inability to engage in any kind of discussion or interchange of ideas bothered her. She never mentioned her concerns to him because how could plain, undeserving Marcia dare to make demands upon a handsome male for whose attentions she should be grateful? However, she did complain about his sullenness to her mother, whose reaction was predictable.

"So what if he doesn't talk much? He's a doctor. And he's so handsome. What more could any girl want? Men are like that. You want conversation, call me!"

Like all medical students, Richard was work driven and exhausted a good deal of the time. In order for them to see each other, it seemed more convenient to have Marcia move into his apartment where she could take care of the household needs more easily than he could, since she just had a nine-to-five job. Their life became a routine of see-you-sometimes, supper and sex as his schedule allowed. As the year went on, the required care and feeding of Richard plus her job made it more difficult for Marcia to find time to study for retaking the M-CAT. The continued pressure from her mother didn't help.

"Why bother with med school—it will be years out of your life, and even if you do get in, how do you know that Richard will wait? What about children? You want to have a family before you're too old. Marry him, and he'll be the doctor in the family."

Marcia longed to be a physician, to have the status, self-satisfaction, sense of personal achievement and security that the M.D. degree symbolized to her. She was not deeply in love with Richard, but their sex life was good, and they had developed an easy compatibility that was pleasant. If she passed this up, how did she know she would ever find another man who might want to marry her? And isn't being married and a mother the real measure of a woman's success? Unequipped with an ego to counter her mother's barrage of corrosive propaganda, Marcia began to believe that marriage to Richard would be the sensible fulfillment of any girl's dream. When her younger brother called with great excitement to say that he had just been accepted by the medical school she had her heart set on, Marcia felt her destiny was confirmed, and she and Richard were married.

Three years later, Marcia had a baby. Anyone who ran into her mother was treated to an unfurled six-pack of baby pictures accompanied by her triumphant trumpeting that her son was a doctor and her daughter a doctor's wife. She was totally fulfilled. But what about Marcia?

Marriage works well between two people who love and like each other and do not mind the overlooking of irksome differences required of a successful relationship. When either element is missing, however, the going is rocky. In an article published in the *New York Times*, Patricia Volk wrote, "There isn't a woman I know who hasn't dreamed of killing her husband....The person you live with...have babies with...is often the person you like least in the world."

Marcia did not like Richard. He was a withholding person who could sit for hours at a dinner table of chattering people and not utter a word. She rarely knew what he was thinking and began to care less. Furthermore, he was a doctor, which automatically creates problems in the marriage department.

In Cynthia's book, *Doctors' Wives: The Truth About Medical Marriages*, she pointed out that men who are doctors are usually obsessive-compulsive individuals who, in order to attain the grades required for medical-school admission, single-mindedly drive themselves scholastically and thereby sacrifice the normal development of interpersonal skills along the way, making them inept and immature in social situations. Since the donning of the magic white coats instantly endows them with godlike qualifications in the eyes of patients and patients' families, they never have the need to develop the social facet of their personalities. All too often, they become arrogant and inflexible in all relationships. We learn how to act from signs of approval and disapproval elicited from others and tend to adjust our behavior to get the most possible positive reaction we can. After all, most of us want to be liked.

Doctors say what they damned please and in any way they please because who's going to call them jerks? We are fearful of offending the great man who controls our survival or that of a loved one and would never dare to complain about his insensitivity, or crassness, or frequently tactless cruelty. In normal social interaction, a person who speaks crudely or hurtfully is usually made aware of his gaffe immediately, and if he has any sense and wants to be invited again, he cleans up his act at once and learns from the experience. But who's going to teach niceness to a doctor? No matter what he says and how he says it, no one dares criticize him. Everyone treats him with respect so he goes through life with the misconception that he is a perfect charmer.

When Cynthia's husband, David, was hospitalized in intensive care for some months, every doctor, intern, resident—anyone in a white coat—who walked into the room was greeted with reverence for he and he alone could give some word as to the patient's condition at that moment. They never seemed to realize the importance their even casual words or attitude held for the frightened family and would sometimes just vent their bad moods by saying something that conveyed anxiety rather than hope. They had no concern or even awareness of the effect of their comments or actions, until one time, David erupted when the young doctor trying to put in an IV kept piercing his arm unsuccessfully looking for a suitable spot. David finally pulled his arm away and snarled, "Leave me alone—go and practice on a doll!" The nurses paled although one did hide a smile. No one talks to a doctor that way!

Richard fit the above profile in every detail, and Marcia was miserable. But the insecurity that had dogged her all her life prevented her from admitting that she might be anything less than happy. After all, hadn't she achieved all the elements of successful womanhood...a husband, house, and baby? She even had the money to live in the luxurious style she had longed for as a youngster. Her self-deception went on until she attended a college reunion with two friends she had not seen since she and Richard moved to another state where he found a practice that suited his needs.

The two young women were happy to see her and hear all about her life. One was an investment banker and the other an engineer, and both exuded the confidence and pride of women who had achieved their goals and were contented with themselves. They had comfortable apartments, dressed well and traveled frequently both on vacations and business and had active social lives. The implicit assumption about reunions is that the only people who attend are those who are successful and/or gorgeous. Nobody goes to flaunt failure, which is why everyone returns from those affairs with the inevitable comment about how wonderful everyone looks. Of course, losers never come; only the winners show up. Marcia fully expected to be regarded as the winner of the three. After all, she alone had achieved all the accouterments of female success: marriage (to a doctor, yet), a baby, and a house. What more could any woman want? To her disquiet, they oohed and aahed over the pictures of her baby and house without displaying any signs of envy and then went on to tell her about their lives, the creation and completion of important business deals, decisions that affected millions of people and dollars, involvement in research and development of advanced technological breakthroughs. She found herself countering with tales of Richard's accomplishments.

Marcia felt dispirited that night and barely spoke to her husband, but he never noticed. She was now thirty-five, living with a man who gave her merely the bare bones of a pleasurable existence. But whose fault was that? She looked at him and realized that the person in the room she liked least at that moment was herself.

Marcia had accepted the mores of her mother and women of past generations even though she had choices that they did not. Her own insecurity and lack of ego led her to buy into their pitch without examining its fraudulent basis. Years ago, women were forced to define themselves by their husbands' achievements because they were not allowed to strive for the same pinnacles. It was customary for a woman to defer to the man's need for education because the couple knew that he could make the most of it. So she would give up college in order to put him through whatever school he needed, secure in the knowledge that she would ultimately bask in the benefits of his status. But today the barriers are down, and she has the opportunity to be whatever she wants and no longer must be consigned to a derivative existence.

Years ago, a woman who wanted a career in medicine rarely dared to be a doctor, instead becoming a nurse; the woman who longed to be a lawyer became a legal secretary. The only way to achieve a position of prestige was to marry it. The women who were strong enough to counter convention and pursue professional careers and sometimes chose to eschew the need for husbands were regarded as admirable, but somewhat lacking because they were not wives and mothers. Marcia had swallowed this old line (her mother's) and as a result suffered from a sense of lost self-identity and could-have-been achievement. Everything in life is a tradeoff—but did she make the right one for her?

Keep your eyes wide open before marriage, half shut afterwards.
—BENJAMIN FRANKLIN, POOR RICHARD'S ALMANAC

8

THEY WANTED TO MARRY IN THE WORST WAY...AND THEY DID

SHE HAS REACHED the pinnacle, the fulfillment of the female America dream...she's married. She is permitted to be smug and satisfied because she is now regarded as a valuable Woman and at least in her mother's eyes, more successful than her friend who is a vice president of Morgan Stanley but still piteously single. She should be happy. So why isn't she?

We marry for a myriad of reasons, but mostly because it is expected of us and we have been instructed that the family unit is the basis of our society and only by conforming to that construct will we be accepted, fulfilled, and consequently happy. We are also given to understand that, as with any convention, those who do not follow the rules will be "Outsiders," forever forced to deal with questions. But isn't it preferable to endure the annoyance of raised eyebrows rather than the pain of unfulfilled dreams? The raised eyebrows are on passing faces whose concerns for you are casual, and to trade in your hopes in order to say "yes" to the careless questions "Are you married?" is foolish to the point of tragic.

CHOICE...THE MAGIC WORD

THE DIFFERENCE BETWEEN years ago and today, between then and now, is the wonderful element of choice...choice when to marry, whom to marry, or if to marry. No longer is there a need for a young woman to obsess because she is single and grab the guy who's available when panic strikes. She can now enjoy the luxury of evaluating what is offered by marriage and make a decision based on her needs rather than those of pressuring parents or conformist-demanding society. Security in her own value as a person, plus the ability to support herself comfortably, give her the license to disregard the marriage license as the only acceptable route.

Unfortunately, many young women today profess to believe in the importance of what is called self-actualization and go so far as to pursue professional careers but never manage to kick the conditioning that inculcated them with the belief that the only true arena of success for women is the home and that no matter what they accomplish elsewhere, they have failed as females unless they are married. Instead of reveling in the sense of satisfaction to which their achievements entitle them, they roil in self-doubt because they are single. Instead of enjoying the day-to-day pleasure derived from stimulating work activity, they denigrate its total importance as compared to the suddenly ennobling and unreachable state of matrimony and motherhood that they forget mired their mothers in mediocrity and drudgery.

They have earned parity positions that should bring them pride and pleasure. Instead, they read every daily wedding announcement with envy and suffer a sense of failure because their names are not there. Torn with jealousy over friends' marriages, they never bother to examine the often miserable realities of such existences as compared to their own. Never mind that one friend married into an emotional wasteland and another wed because of financial need. They got wedding rings, didn't they? And so these self-flagellants become obsessed with wedlock as a state of grace. They want to get married in the worst way, and they do.

THE POWER OF NEGATIVE THINKING

PAULA WAS AN attorney, the first in her family to go on to a higher degree. Pretty, with an engaging vitality, she had a highly responsible position in the trusts-and-estates department of a mid-sized law firm that paid her a very good salary. She had her own apartment in a downtown neighborhood filled with young professionals. She shared rentals on a ski lodge in the winter and a beach house in the summer and took vacations intermittently. She was attractive and gregarious, and finding men had never been a problem for Paula. She had a succession of friendships, relationships, and affairs, and lived with a man for a year before they decided upon an amicable parting. Her job was stimulating, her life was busy and rewarding, and she had the freedom of doing whatever she wanted whenever she wished, but an epiphany occurred when she reached thirty that suddenly destroyed any further possibility of enjoying her formerly totally satisfying existence.

"My God, I'm thirty and not married. Maybe I'll never get married. Maybe I'll be an old maid like poor Aunt Elsa, and everyone will feel sorry for me. What am I doing?...I'd better find a husband fast."

Paula panicked and became an absolute neurotic on the subject until her friends became disgusted with both her conversation and behavior. She ran an ad in the "Personals" column of the local city magazine and met Arthur, a pleasant, if unimaginative, man of thirty-six who was also seeking a "meaningful relationship," and they started seeing each other steadily.

Arthur was a classic JE, junior executive, who held a middle-management job in a major consumer-product corporation and thought that the epitome of ecstasy was to exceed last month's sales quota. Paula found him pleasant, attractive, but boring. She complained to her friends that sex and conversation fell far short of stimulating and that he and she did not enjoy the same things.

Paula came from a blue-collar background where paintings were bought to go with the furniture and vacations meant RV trips with the whole family. Paula had become eagerly upwardly mobile and was hungry to improve her tastes and cultural horizons. Whereas she had previously purchased clothes from popular chain stores, her wardrobe now came from high-fashion shops. She visited museums, bought tickets to the ballet, theater, and concerts. Arthur's idea of entertainment was, like her father's, a movie Saturday night and watching TV football on Sunday. Paula was enriching her life by reaching up. Now with Arthur, she was reaching back down.

Not only was Paula hysterical about impending spinsterhood, she was also fearful of infertility. "How do I know I can ever have babies?" she wailed to her friends. So she decided to test her childbearing ability by not using contraception and then found herself in the mixed-emotional state of pregnancy. She was glad that she could conceive, but unwilling to concede to a marriage with Arthur. So she told him nothing and had an abortion.

Then he decided that they should live together and see how they got along. Since she had by far the nicer apartment, he moved into her place. Time and proximity did not raise her opinion of Arthur. She still found him dull and far below her level of intelligence and self-expectations. But he was nice, and more important, willing to get married.

Ever in pursuit of improvement, Paula sought and got an important position in the legal department of a major company located just outside her city. Not only did the job pay extraordinarily well, but also it offered perks that made Arthur's eyes glitter. To a company man like him, success is measured by benefits, and marriage to Paula meant that he, too, could participate in the bonanzas of corporate paternalism. He began to press for a wedding. Paula was still reluctant to commit herself to a lifetime of mediocrity and balked. But then Arthur pointed out how commuting to the new job would be a chore, whereas buying a house in the suburban area near the company would not only be more convenient, but would enable them to take advantage of the marvelous mortgage terms offered by the corporation. How could they possibly pass up such a wonderful opportunity? Paula was still hesitant. But then, within one month, her younger sister became engaged, and her widowed mother announced that she was going to marry an old friend who had recently lost his wife. That did it.

PAULA DROPPED OUT of sight and lost contact with all her old friends. Months later at Christmas, everyone received cards and angry phone calls asking how come they hadn't called her so that she could inform them that she and Arthur had eloped, bought the house, spent a one-week honeymoon in the Poconos, and had already completely furnished their home in color-coordinated suites as featured in the TV advertisements of the local department store, all financed by low-interest loans offered by Paula's new employer.

Her friends were hurt that she had left them out of such major moves and annoyed by her haranguing accusations of their failures to keep in touch when it was actually she who had removed herself. They realized her anger was really a manifestation of self-reproach and that her longtime reluctance to call was to defer facing their inevitable disapproval and disappointment with her. Each phone call ended with the promise of a future invitation to her new house...which they and she knew would never come.

ALLOWING YOURSELF TO be stampeded into marriage because of external forces rather than internal needs is foolish and can only have an unhappy ending. There is no reason today for any woman to "settle" for life with a husband she does not love and like. Given the fact that even when those elements are present, there are no guarantees that the marriage will work, why further hamper your chances for success by starting with such a major handicap?

STRANDED IN MATRIMONY

SALLY WAS A thirty-three-year-old director of a day-care center who had recently completed a master's degree in education. She did not make a tremendous amount of money since the field is not a high-paying one, but she had always lived simply and had little desire for luxuries. Sally was very happy in her job, she loved working with children. Her small apartment was nicely furnished with pieces taken from her parents' house when they moved to Florida, and she shared it with Becky, a lovable floppy dog with the same placid disposition as her owner.

Sally had a large network of good friends with whom she spent most evenings. Soft spoken and slow moving, she exuded a calmness that was pleasant and somehow reassuring. She disliked dating and preferred long-term relationships like the one she had for two years with Jordan, a brash, immature boy seven years her junior whom everyone was happy to see finally ejected from her home.

Even though Jordan's departure was her choice, Sally missed his presence. Albeit irritating, he was someone. And she needed someone. Sally had no immediate family in the area and not much of one anywhere. Just after her parents moved to Florida, her father died, and her mother subsequently remarried. Sally had a disaffected brother who lived in Europe and with whom she had no relationship at all. Sally was alone and longed for family. It was time to get married and create one.

She noticed an attractive man in her apartment building around whom she built a romantic mystique. Her friends shook their heads at Sally's almost teenage obsession with this mystery man with whom she finally arranged a meeting. He was a freelance industrial designer with the same laid-back personality as Sally's, and they started seeing each other. Ron was hard working and forever weary. He would come over to her house ten o'clock at night after working all day and evening, and fall asleep on the floor watching TV.

Their relationship became steady, yet unlike romances where passion and need for each other pulls the partners together every waking moment, there were weeks when their sole contact was by phone because he was too busy or tired to see her. Her friends were puzzled by Sally's acceptance of Ron's absences and almost phlegmatic behavior when they were together and shocked when she told them that she intended to marry him.

After a year of building his dependence on her for whatever small amount of female companionship he needed, she pulled the old squeeze play and announced that he must declare his serious intentions or she wanted out. She told him that she was thirty-three and wanted to get married and have children, and if he could not agree to those terms, they were finished. In any "either/or" ultimatum, there is danger that the result won't be your choice. It's a risk that is easier to take when you do not have a heavy emotional investment in the outcome. Sally was sanguine because she knew that if it would not be Ron, she would seek someone else. It was the moment and not the man that was all important. She won, and they were wed three months later.

Upon Sally's advice, Ron gave up the uncertainty of freelancing and found a job with a design firm located in an outer suburb. Since Sally's master life plan included a house, they bought one in a town located fifty miles from the city but near Ron's office.

Sally became pregnant almost immediately and continued to commute to her city job, which involved almost two hours of convoluted connections of trains and buses. They both left early in the morning, and she came home exhausted every evening and usually did not see Ron because he stayed at the office until very late. His weekends were spent in the basement where he was building a studio to enable him to bring home unfinished work.

Although they lived together, they seemed to be as separated as before their wedding. They saw so little of each other and talked so rarely that they had little chance to develop the understanding and intimacy that must be the basis of a happy and lasting relationship.

Sally had married because she wanted someone to share her life, and yet now she found herself lonelier than ever before. Her friends were unwilling to make the big trek to her house, so she rarely saw them. Her old pleasure of long chats on the phone was severely curtailed by Ron's carping at the size of their phone bills. She tried to find new friends and activities in the area, but found they had made the major error of basing their decision to buy a house merely on the building without considering the neighborhood.

It was a working-class community of nice, solid people with whom she had absolutely nothing in common. She felt isolated and trapped, and longed to talk it over with her husband. Unfortunately, he wasn't there, and the rare moments they had together involved financial discussions and his lectures on the need for economy in order to meet their growing responsibilities and expenses now that a child was on the way. She had always known that Ron was serious and heavy in his approach to life, but she hadn't realized what a drag it would be to live with someone with such a negative fearful view.

One evening when they managed to have dinner together, she brought up the subject of names for their baby and began suggesting a few, all of which he vetoed.

"How about Samuel? It's a nice name, it was my father's name."

"It's too Jewish," answered Ron.

Sally was stunned. Their religious difference had never seemed important, and suddenly the fact that she was Jewish and he Protestant became an issue that could affect the attitudes and upbringing of their child.

"Who is this man I married?" she began to wonder and, "Can I spend the rest of my life with such a person?"

There are always doubts in the early stages of a marriage. It is the critical time when you learn to accept weaknesses and appreciate strengths. What gets you through is love and a subconscious balancing of the good and the bad. Sally loved Ron, but it was not the overwhelming passion that either blinded her or compensated for the negatives of which there were many. However, the baby was imminent, and that became the most important thing in her life.

After the birth of their son, Sally stayed home for a month and then resumed her old job, taking the baby with her. Working in a day-care center made it a natural since there were facilities for feeding, diapering, and coping with an infant's needs. But the daily trip back and forth became even more onerous as she now carried a baby on her back. She adored her son, but soon realized that he was her baby, not theirs. Ron took little interest in the child and regarded the infant as her total responsibility—that was woman's work.

When the baby was three months old, Ron suddenly announced that he had quit his job and taken a lease on his old studio back in the city, which meant that he, too, would be commuting for three hours daily. Since he was starting a business, more time and dedication than ever would certainly be required.

Sally was heartsick. She had isolated herself in this stupid faraway house for his convenience, and now he had negated the entire basis for her sacrifice. If there had been any glimmer of hope before that his workload would eventually ease up so that they could spend time together, this new move wiped out the possibility. The fact that he never considered consulting his wife before taking such a major career step was further proof to her that their concepts of love, sharing, and parenthood were miles apart. When she entered the marriage, she was ready to accommodate to Ron and expected the same consideration from him.

Going over their short marital history, she saw that he had given nothing to the relationship and was living exactly as he had when he was single with the added advantages of built-in maid and sex service. He had conceded to her pressure to marry because he had little to lose. She had made the down payment on the house with money she had inherited from her grandmother, so his investment was nil. She bore the baby and took full charge of him, and Ron had the pleasures of a nice home and total domestic services. But what was in it for Sally? She felt betrayed; she felt sad; she felt stupid.

Perhaps she had been overly affected by the media hype about surveys that make a big to-do about women's diminishing chances for motherhood as the years roll on. What made age thirty-three the inviolate cutoff date? Why did she allow the sound of the ticking of the so-called biological clock to drown out the discordant noises from Ron that would have alerted her to his unsuitability as a husband? She wanted marriage because it seemed to present the pattern of life she desired. But was this a romantic vision or a real one? Her image of marriage was based on her family, her childhood, a split-level with mom in the kitchen and dad mowing the lawn. But these recollections were purely from a child's point of view. How much did she actually know about her mother's feelings? It never dawned upon her to consider whether her parents were happy, they were just there and married. Her father's retail business kept him busy days, evenings, and Saturdays; wasn't her mother lonely? Did she like being married? Did her father fill her mother's needs, and what were her needs anyway? Sally could not remember cross words between them, but then she didn't remember any words between them.

Sally had reached conclusions about marriage that were based on faulty research. Subconsciously she reasoned that marriage must be the only way to live, else why did her mother marry again shortly after her father died? She should have realized that her mother had no other choice. That was her job title—wife—that's all she knew how to be, and when she lost one job, she just went out and found another. But Sally had options and did not have to accept emotional neglect and punitive living conditions. Her parents' arrangements whereby he gave at the office and she gave at home may have worked for them, but not for Sally.

If Sally had thought things through, she might have realized that no longer was marriage the only lifestyle available to women.

All sorts of satisfactory household arrangements exist that proclaim societal attitudes of incredible *laissez-faire.*

SALLY WANTED A home and child, and she actually provided both for herself. As she learned, there's more to fathering than fertilization, and having a man around the house doesn't always mean companionship. Unmarried motherhood might have been a viable alternative for Sally. Wasn't she actually functioning as a single parent anyway?

DISTRUST, DESPERATION, AND DISASTER

HOW MUCH SHOULD you give up for marriage? Your identity? Your dignity? Your sense of self-worth? I'm sure you are answering these questions no, no, and no. Right? So why do seemingly accomplished women sign punitive prenuptial agreements giving up all their rights? Do some women want to get married so badly that they will accept any terms just for the ring?

We are sorry to say that the answer is too often yes. Our society negotiates everything and changes it at will. Marriage is supposed to be an emotional and financial partnership based on trust. What does a one-sided prenuptial say? It says, "I don't really trust the person from the get-go, but I'll get married anyway." So with a prenuptial agreement, the man expunges the threat of being duped into marriage, and the woman can have the ring even though she has given up the illusion of a lasting relationship even before the ceremony.

So what is the point of entering into such a marriage? The point is that some women still believe that being married is more important than self. It is time that these women consider the alternative, having a relationship without the ties that unbind.

The fact that you are willing to negotiate your divorce before you marry should tell you something about your mate, yourself, and your future.

Many a woman enters into these arrangements to cement a relationship that will make her a mom. Then, she has children and stays home with them, gives up her career and is forced to ask her husband for every nickel needed to run the home.

The strong independent woman she developed herself into is nullified. Even worse, should she find that she or he wants a divorce, she not only has signed away her rights to support, but has also possibly put herself behind the eight ball where her children are concerned. Here she is eight, ten, twelve years into being a stay-at-home mom and out of the work force; she is stale as a wage earner and can't provide a home for her children on a par with the father. Now what?

Hindsight is twenty-twenty, but women blinded by the light of the wedding ring should think ahead: "What if we are married for ten or fifteen or twenty-five years, and what if there are children?" We are rarely given a glimpse into the future. Should you marry a man who feels he should never have any obligation to you, no matter how long you've been married?

Both parties have a legitimate interest in protecting assets they had before the marriage. But think long and hard about why you're signing this document and what it will mean in legal and emotional terms, now and in the future.

I'LL SIGN ANYTHING TO BE MRS.

MOLLY'S FRIENDS THOUGHT she was nuts. Attractive, smart, educated, she had fallen for Henry, a man who treated her, and everyone else, like a subordinate species. The fact that he had created and built two businesses into multimillion-dollar enterprises made her see him as some sort of desirable superbeing, and she pursued him mercilessly. They both had apartments in the city, and when he bought a luxurious weekend home in the environs, she bought a small cottage nearby. She would throw parties and invite him; sometimes he accepted and then never showed up. She would phone him constantly and inveigle him into dates, which he often broke. Henry was a control freak, and Molly's friends were disgusted with the way she allowed him to demean her. "He treats you like crap," said one of her close friends. "Don't you have any pride, for God's sake?"

But the big problem was that Molly wanted to have children. She was thirty-eight, the clock was ticking, and she saw Henry as masculine, strong minded, and rich, the perfect candidate to be her husband and father of her children. She thought she loved him. Henry was fifty with a mother who liked Molly and wanted grandchildren. So finally, with pressure from mom and pushing from Molly, he agreed to marry her.

To Henry, getting married to Molly was not just a matter of sharing his life and future with her, it was giving her possible personal and fiscal power over him. He would not allow himself to be put into that position without protecting his assets from future risks. So he had his lawyer draw up a prenuptial agreement. Molly was so overjoyed that he had finally consented to marry her and so desperate to avoid displeasing Henry that she signed the papers, barely reading them and without even taking the essential step of having them reviewed by her own attorney.

One year later, they had a daughter and the following year, a son and then another daughter. Molly finally had the family she craved—but not the loving, life-sharing husband she dreamed of. They lived well, took the kids to Disneyland frequently, skiing in Colorado in the winter, and sent the children to fine private schools. But where was the companion she expected, perhaps foolishly? Henry did not like people and refused to allow her to entertain and use all the beautiful china and crystal she had accumulated as wedding gifts. He denigrated all her friends and their neighbors and considered none of them worthy of spending time with. Molly's life became totally run by Henry's dislikes, which were many. His complete control extended to their marital financial arrangements.

He refused to have a joint bank account, so she had to ask him for money and he could audit her expenditures. To her dismay, she watched her children develop an arrogant sense of entitlement as Henry bought them every piece of electronic equipment as it came on the market and the girls only the most expensive designer clothing as befitting, as he saw it, the children of a successful man. After ten years, she decided she had enough and wanted a divorce. She went to a tough matrimonial attorney who looked over her prenuptial agreement and then at her in shock.

"You are an intelligent, educated woman. How could you have signed such an agreement? Even a first-year-out-of-law-school lawyer would not have allowed you to sign this." She shamefacedly admitted she had no lawyer.

"You signed away alimony. You signed away any claim to his investments, businesses, and property. All you can get is child support—assuming you get custody."

Molly fought for custody and won, which gave her child support so that she was able to move with the children into the small cottage she owned in town. She got a low-paying job near home and managed to live frugally.

After one year, when the children returned from the expensive summer camp Henry had sent them to in Maine, they announced to Molly that they wished to live with their father. They hated her little house, they hated having to share bedrooms, they hated having to pinch pennies—they wanted to return to their luxurious rooms in dad's lovely big house. Henry had managed to instill his values in them, whereby people are judged by possessions and wealth, and he made them ashamed to bring their fancy private-school friends to the humble cottage.

Henry went back to court, and with the children now old enough to express their living preferences, he was awarded full custody. Molly had prescribed visitations and no more child support.

MANIPULATING A MAN INTO MARRIAGE— A SLIPPERY SLOPE

THERE ARE PEOPLE who see life as a battleground that you must fight your way through. Passivity makes you a pushover, so they manipulate people and situations in order to achieve their goals. In business, such tactics can make you a winner, but in private life, it will make you an ultimate loser.

You have been seeing a man for months, maybe years, and you want to get married, but can't get him to move. You hint, but he doesn't pick up on it because either he's perfectly happy with things as they are or he's scared of making a commitment. It's an old story, and many a happily married woman will tell you how she had to give a subtle little push in order to get him to the altar. The key words here are "little" and "subtle." The manipulator who comes on strong may get her way initially, but at what price? She may give him an ultimatum—marry me or else—but she has to be ready to accept total rejection and his choosing the "else." Or he may decide to go along with her demand, then always harbor resentment at the way she pressured him into the situation, thus dooming the marriage.

But the real risk is that she continues to use manipulation throughout their lives in order to get her way. It worked once, why not forever? Because such tactics weaken with overuse and inevitably will fail, as will the marriage.

LET'S MAKE A DEAL...OR NOT

GLORIA WORKED FOR a large department store and had reached the position of head buyer due to her skill in negotiating suppliers into making excellent deals. She was thirty-four, had grown up in a small town in Michigan, and now lived in an apartment in midtown Manhattan in New York City. She had a busy fulfilling life and had all she wanted except for a husband and children.

She met Don at a dinner party one evening and they began dating. He was forty-five, an engineer with an offbeat approach to life that she, who considered herself a practical realist but whom others saw as a rigid bore, found charming and attractive. She decided he was the man she wanted to be her husband and the father of her children.

Don lived in the suburbs to be near his job with a large international company. He was suddenly transferred to the firm's New York City office to head a specific project that required round-the-clock shifts, and unfortunately, he was assigned the night hours. When he bemoaned to Gloria about the inconvenience of having to travel one hour each way to and from work, and now had to live crazy hours that turned his night into day, she had a brainstorm. She saw a way to bring him into her life.

"Why don't you stay at my apartment during the week?" she asked him. "It's only two blocks from your new offices. I have this big couch, and I'm at work all day, and the place is empty."

It was a no-brainer: Don flipped for the idea, and that began a new routine for them. They spent the weekends together and during the week had the strange intimacy of living in the same place at different times. They would leave each other food in the refrigerator although Gloria left him meat loaf, stew, and other tasty dishes that showcased her domestic abilities while he would leave her empty cartons of ice cream and half-filled cake boxes that showed his bizarre side, which with her small town humor, seemed to demonstrate his wit and sophistication. She became more and more determined to get him to marry her, but hints did not reach him at all.

Don had grown up in one of the most depressed neighborhoods in Bridgeport, Connecticut, the only child of poor immigrant parents. Their life was a struggle for survival that allowed no time or place for demonstrations of love and caring for each other or their son. The way he saw it, marriage was a highly unsatisfying arrangement. Don's career now gave him the style of living he had always dreamed of and that marriage would only destroy. Of course, there was no way a handsome man of forty-five would have lived and socialized in New York City without having been hit upon by women longing to marry, but he had carefully managed to avoid entanglements by the simple method of leaving the relationship when the pressure got too heavy. However, he had never met up with a relentless pursuer like Gloria.

After almost a year of their, to Don, highly satisfactory living arrangement, Gloria announced that she had been offered a great job in a store in San Francisco and was going to move out west. It was now November, and she had to give her answer by December

1 in order to start in January. She told him she hated to leave because she was in love with him (a word he never dared to say for fear it might lead to unwanted entanglement), but the only way she would stay was if he married her. She had received the job offer months before, but held off telling him in order to force him to make a fast, now-or-never decision.

One of the basics of this strong-arm tactic is to never issue an ultimatum unless you are willing to face the downside of rejection. Gloria knew that, but decided to take the risk as she was no longer willing to accept this fun-and-games relationship that he could undoubtedly go on with forever but that for her would lead nowhere. She also knew how to use the pressure of time, so she gave him a deadline for his decision: two weeks, yes or no.

Don was stunned. Other relationships that he had severed had been easy. He had never been in love with any of the women, and he wasn't sure he felt any differently toward Gloria. But this was not just a case of feelings; it was giving up a highly satisfactory lifestyle. She had skillfully made him dependent on her, and he was loath to give it all up.

He pondered the pros and cons. He wasn't a kid, she was attractive, and they enjoyed being together. It was pleasant having someone take such care of him. The fact that she was wildly in love with him and would do almost anything to please him was very flattering. He knew he did not feel the same way about her, but he thought perhaps falling in love was an unrealistic myth, and this might be as good as it gets. She made a lot of money, and he made a lot of money. Together they could have a luxurious life. Maybe it was time.

So on December 15, they got married at City Hall and had a wedding dinner at a restaurant attended by only both sets of very happy parents—"Thank God, at last." The wedding picture showed a glowing jubilant bride and an unsmiling groom who looked like he had stumbled into the wrong party.

For two years, things were great, and Don began to congratulate himself that he had made the right decision. They traveled, went to theater, opera, ballet—all Don's interests. Then one evening, Gloria hit him with the bombshell.

"I'm pregnant. We're going to have a baby."

His face turned stony. "Oh no, we're not. I told you I never wanted kids."

He had. But totally confident in her manipulative talents, Gloria felt she would change his mind when the time was ripe. The debate went on for days, but he was adamant.

"Either you have an abortion, or I'm out of here," he said with such utter finality that she finally realized she had hit something she had never before encountered—an impenetrable stone wall. He told her he was very happy with their marriage and free life and was unwilling to give it up. He hated his childhood and always retained the image of how the burden of parental responsibility wore heavily upon his never-smiling father. He could not see what children would add to their lives, but rather only what they would subtract.

Many women would not have yielded, but Gloria had such confidence in her ability to convince anyone of her point of view that she felt perhaps it was only a matter of poor timing. She would give in now, but come back in a year after giving him months to contemplate the guilt she would make him suffer. He took her to the doctor, and she had the abortion.

The following year, she once again became pregnant. But this time, she was prepared.

"I'm pregnant. I am going to have a baby—your baby. I'm getting too old to expect this to happen again. I will not give up this child."

Again he refused to budge. No children. No way. This time she was prepared with a new tactic.

"I'll make you a deal. Why not wait until the baby is born, and after you've see him or her, if you still feel you don't want to be a father, the baby and I will leave, and you'll never have to see us again."

He looked at her grimly. "I'm on to your manipulating techniques, Gloria. You assume I'll fall in love with the baby at first sight and get hooked. But you're wrong. Decide now—it will be me or your child."

She did not believe him. He drove her to the hospital for the birth and brought her and the baby home. When she got there, she found he had removed all his belongings. He dropped her off and left immediately. The divorce papers followed.

Two years later, she learned he had remarried a highly successful and cultured executive, and they led the free, busy New York life Don craved. But three years later, when Gloria's son was a delightful five-year-old, she found out that Don's second wife had left him—for a woman. Gloria didn't know whether to laugh or cry.

The choice of a point of view is the initial act of a culture.
—José Ortega y Gasset

9

THE MOTHERHOOD OPTION: NON-MOTHERS & SINGLE MOTHERS

MOTHERHOOD, THE FLAG, and apple pie had always been regarded as the sacred American trilogy...revered and unassailable.

But today, custard and quiche maybe outpoll apple in overall national pie consumption. Women can announce that they do not want children and not be stoned in public. We live in an era where everyone comes out of the closet and admits very personal heretofore private feelings and proclivities without risk of being ostracized.

Thirty years ago, two female friends opted not to have children. One was an attorney and the other a merchandising executive. Because they were such high-powered women, no one dared to question their choice. However, we can still remember two older women who were pitied as failed wives because they had no children. Women who chose to forgo motherhood were disbelieved as people whispered behind their backs: "So I wonder whose fault it is—his or hers."

THE DEATH OF MOMISM

NOW IT'S OUT in the open. Not all women want to be mothers. Not all of them believe that a woman's only route toward the fulfillment of her destiny is to bring up children. Although the maternal urge has always been regarded as a universal female trait, we are now finding out that it is not. Not all women want to have children; recent figures have shown that twice as many couples as ten years ago have decided not to have children.

So why do we still make women who do not have children defend their position? Why do we use the word "childless," which implies that to have a child is the natural state and to be without offspring is to be in some way less? Because as usual, society has not yet caught up with contemporary changes in behavior—but we're getting there.

For those women who do want children, marriage as the necessary means to motherhood has also lost its luster as a lodestar. Wanting to have children is not always connected in women's minds with getting married: Women can have children alone now, after all, and many women who are married when they have a child find that they wind up raising the child alone anyway.

Aside from frequent financial difficulties, many women and children do not find that this is an unhappy way of life at all. The nonmarital birthrate in the United States has risen 24 percent between the early to mid-1990s and the early 2000s. The stigma of "out of wedlock" is virtually gone, and single women who are reaching past what we used to call "childbearing age" and have not found the man they wish to marry can and often do opt to go to sperm donors and have babies.

According to the 2007 National Marriage Project, "America has the highest percentage of mother-only families. Many European nations have a much higher percentage of out-of-wedlock births than we do, but the great majority of these births are to unmarried but co-habiting couples. In America, much more often, children are born to a lone mother, with the father not in residence and often out of the child's life." According to "The Relationship Context of Births Outside Marriage: The Rise of Cohabitation in America" by Lisa Mincielli and Kristin Moore, May 2007, "Nearly half of all extra-marital births in America were of this nature in 2001."

MARRIAGE NO LONGER THE MEANS TO MOTHERHOOD

ERIN, A BEAUTIFUL, willowy, thirty-seven-year-old woman, decided that she wanted to have a child before she was thirty, so at age twenty-eight she bore a son.

"I was not in a relationship at the time nor did any of the past men I'd known strike me as the kind of person I wanted to marry and spend my life with. So I had my baby with the boyfriend I was seeing then. He knew I wanted to be pregnant and he told me that as far as he was concerned it was strictly my affair—and that was fine with me."

Today, her son is a great source of pleasure to her, and she is totally happy with her decision to be a single mother.

"The idea of marriage never entered my mind." As Erin moved into her thirties, she had some long-term relationships, but they never seemed to be the right ones.

"I like being on my own. I'm comfortably happy. Why should I be with someone who makes me and my son even slightly unhappy?

"I like the energy between man and woman, and I sometimes think I would like to fall in love. But these days, I'm in control, and I find that falling in love is based on your desire to fall in love. So maybe I don't really want what could be a disturbing element. I'm very contented with my son and my life, and I can't see where marriage offers me anything except maybe financial help that I could always use. But it's such a risk—I would hate to face the hassle of getting out of it if it's wrong."

Erin has recently gone back to college and discovered she has a flair for computers that can lead to a lucrative career. Since she is totally self-supporting and money is frequently a problem, she is very excited about her future.

"My son is in school all day, and so am I. It's great."

He is a poised child who is active and happy. Erin attributes this to the stability of his home life as contrasted with so many of his friends who have divorced parents. She points out that these children suffer through the bickering and bitterness that is usually concomitant with divorce, and whereas they are never sure where they will be when and with whom, her son always knows his home and mother are dependable certainties.

"I'm independent. I like my life just as it is—I wouldn't want to change a thing," she said with a very contented smile.

As more and more women enter their thirties still not having found the man they wish to spend their lives with, the option to have a child without marriage is becoming more attractive and almost commonplace. If she is financially secure, has her own apartment or house, and wants to share her life with a child but not a man, why not become a single mother?

SINGLE-PARENT STATUS

IN AN ARTICLE about women lawyers in the *New York Times Magazine*, a success story depicted a partner at one of the nation's largest law firms. She had never married, a circumstance she said was linked to the demands of her career. Unwilling to forgo the experience of motherhood, she adopted an infant daughter and then a son. "Family was extremely important to me," she said of her decision to become a single parent. She worried how her partners would react to her single motherhood. Her female colleagues were immediately supportive. As it turns out, her male colleagues did not appear to be fazed by her single-parent status. They lined up outside her office to hold her baby when she returned from maternity leave.

When single parenthood is accepted with such sang-froid by that most conservative of enclaves, the big-city law firm, and is reported openly in the nonsensational media, then you know that the stigma is gone.

More and more luminaries are having babies out of wedlock. The expression "born on the other side of the blanket" is virtually unknown today while the word "bastard" is used for cursing rather than describing illegitimacy, another archaic term.

THE PASSING OF THE "NORMAL HOME"

WE CANNOT RECALL one friend whose parents were divorced when we were children. How many children can say that today? With the current divorce rate hovering around 50 percent, single-parent households are as conventional as mom-and-dad homes. Children tend to dislike being unlike their peers, and where years ago a child of divorce would have suffered from feeling painfully different, today in some neighborhoods, the kids of nuclear families are the rare birds. It's become like Hollywood, where criss-crossing of parents was always prevalent. Remember the old joke of two movie stars' children fighting when one threatens the other, "I'll get my father to beat up your father!" and the other one answers "But my father *is* your father!"

Marriage and motherhood are no longer the necessary combination. Melissa, who was interviewed in a previous chapter and lives with a man whom she has no intention of marrying, stated that she wants children when she reaches her mid-thirties and intends to have them.

"What's the difference to our kids if we are married? We're just 'mom and dad,' just like my parents were. Why would it even enter their minds to ask? Do you remember ever asking your parents if they were married? Besides, by that time, it will be so common that marriage will not even be an issue."

If you have any concern that children brought up with only mothers will be in any way warped, research studies indicated that such children do well in both careers and personal relationships. In fact, boys who spend most of their childhoods with only their mothers have better relationships with women later and are more verbal and less competitive in relationships than boys who grow up with both parents.

Perhaps the prevalence of divorced mothers bringing up sons in fatherless homes may result in a coming generation of kinder and more respectful men. All the women we spoke to who are in this position repeatedly mentioned how they are raising their boys to be considerate, kind human beings, and as one woman said, "I want them to be gentlemen. Opening doors, pulling out chairs for women may seem old fashioned, and were destroyed by the women's lib movement, but I see these gestures not as demeaning women, but rather as showing respect." We noted that these women frequently mentioned how they stressed these values so that their sons would not grow up to be the boors their fathers were.

The decision to have a baby without a live-in father is not one to be taken lightly. Not having another parent to share the problems and pleasures that arise in the raising of a child can result in times when you may feel deprived and torn and wonder whether you have been fair in depriving your child of a so-called normal home. The consolations here may come by your realizing that there is no longer such a thing as a "normal home" since normalcy is determined by numbers, and single-parent homes may be on a par with two-parent families.

Although at the time of crisis, one longs to have another person who shares your concerns to help make critical decisions, it is good to remember that split thinking could be a drawback rather than a boon and that the need to argue with a father over what you and he think is right could be aggravating as well as destructive.

Another factor to be considered in your decision process is the complaints so many married women make about their husbands' lack of involvement in bringing up their children, that many of them find that they are, in effect, "single mothers." The bodily presence of another parent doesn't necessarily mean shared responsibility. Single mothers usually develop a network of relatives and friends who supply the warm family background in which to nurture the growth and development of a child.

Single motherhood may or may not be the route you select, but it is good to know that it is a viable option for your future.

The absurd is essentially a divorce.
—ALBERT CAMUS

10

WHY DIVORCED WOMEN WITH KIDS SHOULDN'T MARRY

"I KNEW I SHOULDN'T interfere—but when I heard Alan yelling at Michelle, I couldn't stand it. He may be my husband, but he's not her father." Those kinds of conflicts inevitably occur when the man of the house isn't the father of the resident children. Clashes become corrosive, and divided loyalties tear a woman apart. Is it worth it?

The process of divorce in itself is painful and destructive to everyone involved, mother, father, and children. When the legalities are completed, the wife can buckle down to the task of rebuilding a family life for herself and the children with the new lineup of single-parent authority. It's a big adjustment for everyone, but in time, things settle into an acceptable routine. The kids find their lives in school and with friends go on much the same. Even though they now see dad on a schedule, the stability of having mom always there keeps them on an even keel.

Before long, the divorce that at first seemed to be a horrible, revolutionary eruption now becomes just another accepted element. After all, lots of kids in school have divorced parents, what's the big deal? In fact, it's kind of nice to have mom all to one's self and not have to share her with dad who was always resentful when she spent the evening helping a hysterical daughter with her term paper ("Help me, Mom. I'm gonna fail, I know it!"), leaving him alone in front of the TV set or angry when she interrupted his preprandial cocktail hour to run out and pick up a son after choir practice ("Why don't you let him walk home or ride his bike? So what if it's raining, he won't melt"). And for sure, no one's going to miss the constant bickering and fighting that made the house a misery.

BUT WHAT ABOUT mom? After the initial relief over the cessation of hostilities and the residual bitterness fades, going to bed alone every night and having no adult at home to share the tales of the day with create a void that needs filling. So she starts dating. At first, the kids are discomforted by the presence of a courting male. Mothers shouldn't have boyfriends, teenagers have boyfriends, babysitters have boyfriends. But mom, it's weird. Then they get used to her going out to dinner or wherever couples go in the evenings.

In time, they become accustomed to the presence of different men. Increasingly, one man seems to be in the house more often, and they sort of get used to having him around. He's not their father, but he's OK. He doesn't bother them; in fact, he tries to be very nice to them, and mom seems to be happier.

Then mom calls the kids together in the living room and tells them that she and what's his name are getting married. Suddenly, they have to face a new eruption. Just when they had adjusted to all the arrangements and convoluted time-sharing confusion that divorced parents create, a new divisive element is being introduced, and they will have to face coping with another person whose status is a puzzlement and whose presence has already changed mom's response to their needs. They are upset, they are scared, they hate the idea, and though he seems like a nice guy, they hate him, too.

This is the atmosphere in which the new marriage gets its start. And if you think the kids' initial antagonism is difficult, wait until the new man moves in.

TWO HOMES CAN BE BETTER THAN ONE

RITA MET MARTIN at a Parents Without Partners meeting. It was two years after a very messy and acrimonious divorce from a neurotic husband who had driven her crazy with demands for attention and rules for behavior that had kept her and her two little daughters in a state of constant turmoil. He had categorically refused to leave their comfortable suburban house until she was driven to take the children and move into an apartment in the area.

Although this was against the advice of her attorney, it was encouraged by her therapist, who knew Rita would crack up if she continued to live with that maniac. The little girls, aged ten and twelve, missed their friends and neighborhood and the space of their own rooms and a large house, but were soon happy to be free of the erratic tirades from a father who demanded neatness and order. And they did have the stability of continuing in the same school.

Rita's job as trust officer for a local bank was interesting and responsible, and she resumed the active social-life network with her childhood friends and relatives whom she had been unable to see during her marriage because of her husband's cantankerous refusal to have anything to do with her family. She missed sex, however, and desired the company of men. So when she heard of this group of people in similar circumstances, she attended a meeting and met Martin, who had recently divorced his wife of twenty-two years.

Rita was forty-one, which was fifteen years younger than Martin. He was the manager of a large local hardware store and like Rita, had lived in the area all of his life. He, too, had two children, but they were in their twenties and off on their own.

Rita was a very controlled, self-contained woman, and she found herself attracted to Martin's outgoing personality and highly emotional reactions to almost everything. Where she cared only about selected people, institutions, and events, he cared about everything and everybody and was forever exploding at one of his children's behavior or inveighing against the activities of the government and writing irate letters to the local newspapers. Like most people who hate deeply, he also loved deeply, and his warmth and affection were a delightful change to Rita, who had been living with an icy husband who had difficulty even saying, "Have a nice day."

They started dating, and her daughters became accustomed to seeing Martin in and out of the house. On weekends when the girls were with their father, Rita and Martin went off to nearby inns, or he stayed over at her apartment and just lazed around and enjoyed sex and the Sunday papers.

Then he asked her to marry him. Rita was hesitant because things were very pleasant and right for her now. Furthermore, from her experience with marriage, she did not see where becoming husband and wife would improve the situation. In fact, she had serious reservations about the many possibilities for wreaking havoc on what was a comparatively smooth and carefree life. But Martin was persistent.

Why not? From where he sat, marriage would be a major upgrade. He lived alone in a small apartment, which was all he could afford after alimony payments. A lifetime of wifely care had made him totally unfamiliar with the kitchen or washing machine, and taking care of his basic living needs presented daily problems. A gregarious man with no real interest other than his work and attending the movies, plays, and dinner parties his ex-wife had arranged for, he found the solitary life was not for him. He was lost and needed the structure and company supplied by a wife.

He pleaded and cajoled, and Rita began to waver. Her first response to his proposal was a resounding no, but Martin's continuous persuasion began to have its effect. His arguments plus the niggling fear that her refusal would ultimately turn him off and lead him to look elsewhere finally made her agree. And so they were married, and Martin happily moved into Rita's bedroom and prepared to perform the role as husband and stepfather.

The first rude awakening came in front of the TV set, a place Martin loved to spend his evenings. When the girls wanted to turn on their favorite programs, he insisted on watching wrestling. Since there was but one set in the house and it was located smack in the middle of the living room, his positioning himself there with the blasting sound he preferred became a major irritant for the entire household. When he walked in one afternoon after school and found them watching a soap opera, he turned off the set in a fury because they should not at their ages be allowed to see the sort of licentious activities that abound on the tube, and their mother was wrong to be so permissive. It was one battle after another.

The conflicts of interest and opinion were bad enough, but even worse was the highly emotional yelling that was Martin's natural response to anything of which he disapproved. This was frightening to the girls who were used to the cold silences and tight-lipped castigations of their father and made them confused and angry. After all, who did he think he was, anyway? He wasn't their father. He was an interloper who had insinuated himself into their home and was trying to take over.

The purchase of another TV set for the girls' room helped somewhat, but his continual presence and vocal opinions on their behavior made the home unpleasant. Since Martin's store was just a few blocks from the apartment, he was home early and dropped in frequently, and the girls felt their lives were being destroyed by this man who always had something to say about everything they did.

Rita used to look forward to coming home after a day at the bank and relaxing with the girls at the kitchen table with a pot of tea while they regaled her with the details of their day's activities. It was a warm, happy time—but now it was destroyed. Instead, she felt she was entering a war zone when she opened the front door. The girls were either sulking in their rooms or, worse, were away studying at friends' houses because they hated their own. Martin was usually ensconced in front of the TV ready to greet her angrily with complaints about her daughters' disrespectful behavior.

"What did I need this for?" she wondered as she sat up at night unable to sleep after another disagreement with Martin about her performance as a wife and mother. Martin was of another generation, and his approach to child rearing was totally different than Rita's. Also, he had sons and regarded daughters as vestal-virgins-in-training who had to be guided and protected from heaven knows what.

Mothering is difficult enough when fraught with the dual guilt of divorce and career; the constant carping of a critic begins to undermine self-confidence and can turn even the firmest parent into a vacillating wimp. Rita began to question everything she thought and did and found herself unable to make even the simplest decisions about the children.

Torn between responsibility to her daughters and to her husband, she began to feel that the good new life she had fought so hard to achieve for herself and her children was in jeopardy. Rita's divorce had been a bitter battle with a vindictive husband. In order to create a stable, happy home for herself and her daughters, she had willingly sacrificed the comfort and security of a well-subsidized life that included a luxurious five-bedroom house and live-in maid, moved to an apartment that was half the size of her house, and went to work. To see everything she had hard won collapsing because of Martin made her wonder if she had not made a terrible mistake.

Rita loved Martin and was truly reluctant to give up on their marriage, but she saw no way that their lives could continue under the present arrangement without doing damage to the carefully constructed happy new life she and her children had just begun to enjoy. The constant friction among them was destroying her relationship with the girls, as well as her love for Martin. Her anger over being forced into the no-win role as referee was changing her from a serene person into an irritable neurotic.

Finally, she realized that she had left one kind of destructive marriage only to enter into another. But there was one major difference. Her first husband was an erratic, oppressive person with whom she could never spend her entire life. But Martin was a kind, loving man who she knew could make her happy, and the relationship was definitely worth saving. If only she hadn't permitted herself to be talked into marriage. She finally came up with what she considered a workable solution and bided her time for the right moment to broach it to her husband.

She waited until the girls were out visiting friends one Friday evening and then sat Martin down in the living room and presented him with a stunning proposition.

She told him that there was no longer any viable possibility that their marriage could survive under the existing conflicted conditions. Even if they moved to a house which might alleviate some of the concentrated intimacy enforced by the close proximity of an apartment, it would not change the rigid stepfather stance Martin had unfortunately assumed. Nor would it alter the fact that he did not approve of her children, and she did not approve of his disapproval. Rita told him that she considered him a wonderful guy and lover, but his flareups and explosions over even small domestic problems had brought a disruptive note into what had heretofore been a placid and happy household.

"I don't want to break up, Martin. I do love you, but I don't know how much longer I will if we keep on this way. I keep thinking about how wonderful it was before. Do you remember how we enjoyed our weekends, what fun we had, how we laughed over dinner? Now all we ever do is argue.

"What I want us to do in order to save our marriage is to go back to living like before. You move back to your apartment, and we'll spend weekends together like before. We'll go out to dinner and places some evenings during the week. But you won't live here. Bring me your laundry, that's fine. You'll even eat over an evening or two during the week the way you used to. You'll always have the comfort and security of knowing that you have a wife to love you, depend upon, to take care of you when you get sick. Look, I know it sounds crazy but I think it will work. Some people have separate bedrooms, we'll have separate apartments. Think about it, when the girls are racing around here blasting their radios or bringing in friends who take over the kitchen, rummage around the fridge, and make popcorn, don't you sometimes really wish you were back in your old nice quiet apartment? Face it, you're fifty-six and have no patience with young kids. Maybe in eight years or so when the girls are in college, we'll live under one roof. But right now, we can do everything together just like a married couple except live together."

After Martin's initial shock wore off, he began to view the proposal calmly. He loved Rita and did not want to give her up. He, too, had come to realize that their life was becoming untenable, but had avoided facing up to the dread alternative. If they broke up, they would have only a past. But if he accepted Rita's proposal, they could have a pleasant present and a certain future. Martin moved back to his old apartment and they started an entirely new living arrangement that turned out to be not only highly satisfactory, but a little exciting, as well.

The concept of two-home relationships is more common than might be imagined. Many women want to preserve their privacy and independence yet want the comfort and reassurance of a dependable ongoing relationship. And why not? It's your life and whatever arrangements work for you and your partner are acceptable today. Some people may consider your lifestyle remarkable, but there are many who will regard it as enviable.

THE RIGHT LOVER IS OFTEN
THE WRONG STEPFATHER

CONSTANCE IS A handsome, blonde divorcee of thirty-eight who lives in a very small town in Vermont with her two sons aged thirteen and fifteen. She is an extremely successful saleswoman for a real-estate company that sells dreams to city folk who long to own a piece of peaceful pastoral respite from the rat race. Her income from commissions last year was $95,000, and this year looks even better.

She owns a nice house that is run efficiently and happily by a local woman who takes care of the boys, sees that they have milk and homemade cookies when they come home from school, usually with a pack of friends, and a hot and nutritious dinner every night. Constance never has dinner with her sons. She is usually too exhausted after a day's work to deal with the rowdy behavior of teenagers, and the boys are too busy with their friends to want to talk to her, anyway. She eats out every night and comes home about 8:00 to help with homework and hear about the boys' day. It's an arrangement that may seem strange to some, but has worked out wonderfully. The boys are active, happy, and doing well in school and Constance is able to pursue her own life and career without the distracting and destructive onus of guilt.

The choice of that house in that town was carefully planned. When her divorce from a ne'er-do-well husband was final, she was left with two small boys and little chance of collecting child support from a man who never held a job longer than six months. Knowing that she would be the sole support of the family, she looked for a career where income was contingent upon input effort because she knew she had the drive and brains to succeed. When she was offered a selling job with the real-estate company where acreage units went for five figures and up and thus earned commissions could become sizable, she knew this was exactly the opportunity she sought.

Fully aware that tremendous amounts of time and energy would have to be devoted to the job in order to produce, she went about making proper provisions for the care and upbringing of her boys. Because she knew she would have to be absent a good deal, she sought and found a small town where neighbors become extended families and front doors are always welcomingly open. Using her total savings, she bought a small house smack in the middle of town so that they would be surrounded by people and activities. And then she found a local woman who was eager to earn a comparatively easy income caring for two boys who were at school all day and a house with no critical madam white-gloving the woodwork.

Constance's well-thought-out plan gave her and her children the kind of solid, secure existence and future she wanted for them. A vital and attractive woman, she had needs for sex and male companionship, which she found with not too much difficulty. The only shadow in what was an otherwise highly satisfactory and happy life was the continually expressed disapproval of her puritanical Scottish-born mother, who lived in another state but still managed to use the telephone, mail, and frequent visits to comment on what she viewed as her daughter's hedonistic life of sin.

"A woman should be married. Divorcing your husband was bad enough. True he was a wastrel, but a good woman could have made something from him. You failed at marriage, and now you are failing as a mother. Leaving those boys alone all day in the care of strangers! They need a mother and a father."

It was a constant litany that annoyed, but did not bruise Constance. Although most of us seek our parents' approval until the day they or we die, Constance had lost respect for her mother's opinions when she was ten years old and received what she considered an asinine answer to the question of who was the "They" who seemed to control the family's behavior. Constance had wanted to wear her new patent-leather Mary Jane pumps, but her mother forbade it because "They" did not wear patent leather until Easter. When her mother could not identify or even describe this all-powerful "They" who were the major force in decisions about what was important, wrong, or right, Constance decided that her mother was a silly woman and she never really listened to her again.

Constance dated a number of men until she met Roger, a widower with no children, who became her steady companion. He owned a thriving, prosperous construction company that he had built from scratch in a field noted for toughness and power. He was a strong-minded and opinionated man, and Constance rather enjoyed his firm unilateral decision making that enabled her to coast along mindlessly in her social life in happy contrast to the stressful problem-solving requirements of her business life.

One weekend, he announced they were flying to the Bahamas, and they did. He was great fun, good company, and the sex was marvelous. He picked her up at home from time to time and got to know her sons. Constance was amused at his tough-guy dealings with the boys and what she jokingly referred to as his "construction crew boss" posture.

Her mother met Roger and was tremendously impressed with him.

"Now there's a fine real man. He'd make a wonderful husband for you and father to the boys. You'd better try to get him to marry you because Lord knows you're not getting any younger and with two sons, who knows when you'll get another chance. A handsome man like that and rich, too, I wonder why he sees anything in you at all what with all the pretty young girls he could probably get."

Constance began to spend a good deal of time with Roger in the lavish apartment he maintained in a nearby city, and their life settled into a pleasant and almost domesticated existence. One day, he told Constance he had decided that it was time that they got married.

"You decided?" said Constance laughing. "How about asking me?"

Roger shrugged since he considered proposing only a foolish formality that would naturally elicit a "yes" answer.

"No," said Constance. "I don't want to get married. I did that already, and it's not for me."

Roger was absolutely shocked. The possibility of refusal had never entered his mind.

"What you did before has nothing to do with now," he said. "Your husband was a loser and good riddance. I'd give you a good life and be a father to your kids."

She looked at him in surprise. "But we have a good life just as it is. And I don't want a stepfather for my sons. Why don't we just keep things as they are?"

Roger was furious. Here he had finally made the big concession and decision to make a major commitment, and he was rebuffed. It was unthinkable. Then he gave Constance an ultimatum.

"I want to get married. I want a home and a wife. So either you say 'yes' or that's it, and we stop seeing each other. Think it over. You'll come to your senses. Don't give me your answer now; save it for next week."

The next time her mother dropped in for a visit, she noticed that her daughter was no longer seeing Roger.

"So he threw you over, did he? Didn't want to marry you, of course, just as I thought. Men! They're all the same."

Constance never bothered to tell her mother that in no way would she ever have considered bringing Roger into her home. He was a fun guy to visit, but she would never subject her sons to his authoritative demands. She could cope with his bullying ways, but her young sons could not. She would have been perfectly content continuing the lifestyle pattern they had established, but considered it unfair to impose the needs of her libido upon her family. At first, she missed Roger and the romance of the relationship, but she got caught up in a big land-development project her firm had just undertaken and soon forgot all about him.

SHE WANTED A MAN...BUT NOT 24/7

AUDREY IS A college professor who lived in the suburbs with her husband and two teenage sons when she had an affair with her next-door neighbor, Ted, who was also married with children. Ted's wife was ill, and he did not want to leave her. When she died and his daughters were in college, he moved to an apartment in the city. Shortly thereafter, Audrey divorced her husband and moved to an apartment in Ted's building.

In no way did Audrey ever again wish to tie her life to a man. She wanted a place for her sons to live during school holidays, where they would feel totally comfortable and at home without the disturbing presence of an outsider who would necessarily have some quasi-authority over their behavior. She did not want to have to deal with a man's needs, demands, and raging id.

She wanted a man; she wanted Ted—but not twenty-four hours a day. She wanted to be able to come home from a particularly exhausting day and have a glass of wine and a bath without saying a word for two hours and not have to face the hangdog look of the hurt husband or rejected resident male. She wanted to spend some evenings and nights with Ted, but not necessarily all of them.

This was ten years ago, and the relationship still flourishes. Friends regard them as a couple and usually invite them together. Ted's daughters know that Audrey is their father's lover, and her sons are aware of the setup, as well. But nobody minds because the relationship in no way inhibits the children's access to their parents, as it would if they shared habitation. In fact, the children are happy that their parents are happy and not alone, thus less of a responsibility. It's the perfect solution because it works for everyone concerned.

Years ago, such a relationship would have been regarded as scandalously illicit, and all family members would pretend it did not exist.

REMARRIAGE IS A FAMILY AFFAIR

A DIVORCED WOMAN who wishes to remarry has only her own needs to consider. But the presence of children introduces totally new elements that can have a life or death effect upon the configuration of the remarriage. Any divorced mother who believes that she can get married and automatically live happily ever after has seen too many TV sitcoms.

There have been numerous books written telling people how to live with stepchildren. A stepfamily arrangement is tough and mined with traps and pitfalls. First we have to deal with the son's Oedipal suffering to see mother sharing a bed with some strange man. It was bad enough to accept the fact that his father had sex with her, but now this creep who isn't worth her pinky? There are bound to be brushes between son and stepfather that may never be resolved.

What about daughter, an acne-ridden teenager who feels like an undesirable, unpopular ugly and has to deal with jealousy of a mother who has attracted and snared not one, but two men? And maybe to compound her feelings of inadequacy and envy, she's even got a crush on the lover-now-husband.

Then we have the "who-is-he-to-take-our-daddy's-place?" resentment when they see this new man moving into dad's bedroom, bathroom, and place at the table.

Women also must face the problem posed by the masculine ego that directs the new resident male to assume the role of head of the household, replete with the need to issue orders and demands at the get-go of the marriage rather than waiting until a relationship develops whereby he has earned the right to do so.

Another major problem is that today's generation of technological whizzes and video-game-playing smart-assed kids is totally different from the father-knows-best children that the stepfather and his siblings were. Grown men today have a hard time dealing with the challenging attitudes kids now exhibit. The foul language that is considered acceptable on TV and in movies has converted children's casual conversations into litanies of curses that would have guaranteed soap-in-the-mouth punishments years ago. Respect for adults is no longer a given, but must be earned. Witness the difficulty teachers suffer in classrooms filled with totally undisciplined youngsters.

And last we have the poor polarized wife/mother torn between the needs of children and husband. She wants her new husband to share child-rearing decisions with her and knows that his position should entitle him to respect and the right to impose discipline. But deep down, she knows that his emotional commitment to the children cannot be equal to hers, which must make her question the motivation and intent of his decisions and disciplinary actions. How can she trust his reactions when she knows they are based only on his needs for comfort and convenience and not on love?

A WORKABLE ALTERNATIVE TO MARRIAGE

VICKI WAS IN love with Carl, and they talked about living together. She had divorced her husband ten years ago and walked out with her two-year-old son and infant daughter on a marriage that she felt was a dreadful mistake. Helped by minimal child support payments, she worked as a saleswoman in a neighborhood clothing store where her children could stop in on the way home from school and visit with her for a few minutes before going home to the apartment that was just a few doors down. Carl was a machinist in a local plant, and they had been dating for a few months and now felt their relationship was ready to move on into a more serious commitment.

Vicki was thirty-seven, and Carl was the same age and had never been married. He liked her children, loved her, and had a pleasant easygoing disposition that Vicki felt would make him a welcome addition to the household. He mentioned marriage, but Vicki ignored it.

"OK," she told him. "You move in, and let's see how it works out. But remember this, you're my friend, your relationship is strictly with me and not the kids. You're not their father, you're not their boss. Only I am. If they do something that bugs you, tell me, and I'll deal with it. They've been brought up to respect grownups so they'll be good kids. So it should all work out fine."

And it did. Relieved of the need to assert a position with the children, Carl just relaxed, and they began to accept him, at first as a nice friend and then as someone to respect and admire whose judgment they sought constantly to the delight of their mother. Rather than having to force his authority upon them, he earned the right to impose it in time.

Five years later, they have developed a warm relationship that is totally undistinguishable from that in any conventional nuclear family. From time to time, Vicki is asked why she and Carl do not marry.

"What for?" she says. "How will that make it better?"

SELECTING A LIFE PARTNER
WHEN YOU HAVEN'T LIVED

"WHY WON'T THE 'In Crowd' accept me?" "Not one boy asked me to the dance!" "I'm not in a single honors class?" She is obviously a failure with a dim future.

Of course. A teenager's frame of reference for success is based entirely on her school experience. How then is she qualified to make a judgment on how and with whom to spend the rest of her life?

When Cynthia was in college, cliques, as usual, ran the place. The students that controlled all class publications—newspaper, yearbook, and literary magazine—ran only pieces written by them. Every one of her submissions was rejected. Today, Cynthia is the author of twelve published books and many magazine articles, and not one of her classmates has ever had anything in print. If Cynthia had accepted their opinions as valid, she would have made the mistake of deciding that a writing career was obviously not in the cards. Life values arrived at by narrow school-world experiences are bound to be inaccurate, and to make a major life decision based on those standards can lead to disaster.

PROUD OF HER BOYS AND HERSELF

TERESA IS AN attractive woman in her forties and has two ex-husbands and two sons.

"I was only nineteen when we got married. He was a star jock at school and became a golf pro."

With a glamorous, handsome husband, she felt she had hit the jackpot. All the bejeweled women at the club where he worked fawned over him and giggled with delight when he wrapped his arms around them in order to demonstrate how to hit the ball properly. All the wealthy successful men at the club to whom he gave lessons admired his skill and envied his fit muscled body and bought him drinks and tipped him generously. Teresa attended club dances with him and reveled in the sophisticated life, which she had never before experienced. She got a job in the computer department of a local company and earned a good salary. The young couple lived well, and life was great.

Then her husband felt he needed the prestige of winning golf tournaments in order to further his professional life, and he entered competitions all over the country. Tiger Woods has sponsors who gladly pick up the tabs, but a novice has to provide his own travel expenses, not to mention costly wardrobe changes.

Soon, his entire income was spent on his travels, and they began to live solely on Teresa's salary. He was away so much that she began to feel lonely. When he returned home always without a trophy, he became irritable as they were both forced to realize that he was a good golfer, but not a great one and was destined to spend his life making a fair, but not lavish living as a club golf pro.

Teresa began to feel used. The partnership she had envisioned marriage would be turned out to be a false hope. She had married the popular jock figure so revered in high school and college, which made her feel successful, but found that in real life the world is populated by over-the-hill jocks, and there are more important standards by which to select a life partner.

After two years, her eyes were opened, and she decided she'd had it. When she discussed the possibility of divorce with her mother, the advice was "Dear, it will get better. Give it a chance."

But of course, it didn't improve and so four-and-a-half-years later, they were divorced. Teresa was now twenty-three, living alone for the first time in her life. Then she met Jack, who was the opposite of her first husband. He had a good career in retailing, made a good living, and was kind and attentive. She fell in love with him. So they decided to live together.

After a highly satisfactory cohabiting year, they both decided they wanted a family and got married. After the birth of their two boys, they worked out a life plan for their family's future. They would live on Teresa's salary and bank Jack's entire income in an account for their retirement and the boys' college. As opposed to her first marriage, Teresa now felt she was an equal partner.

Then she began to notice he was being extremely attentive to other women, especially the young women he worked with. At first she thought it was just flirting, but odd phone calls and business parties to which she was not invited made her suspicious. He traveled a good deal setting up branch stores and would be away for a week at a time and call home maybe only once to find out how she and the kids were doing.

Finally, she blew her top and accused him of infidelity, which he denied vehemently. This began many such fights and accusations that ended up with Jack calling her a "dumb bitch" and other vile epithets. He began to refuse to do his share of home chores and abused her verbally when she asked him to do something as simple as taking out the garbage.

Their life became a misery, but still she held on. She accepted that he was deceitful, but he was the father of her boys, and it was still a marriage. As with most women who are abused, verbally or physically, the desire to keep the family together is so strong that they delude themselves into thinking it was in some way their fault, they had failed him, every marriage goes through some difficulty, and he should be given another chance.

Then one day while he was away, the bank statement arrived for his account—the one that had been set up to secure their future and the boys' college. She had never opened his mail before, but for some reason, decided to read this. To her horror, she saw that the account, which was supposed to be an accumulation of fifteen years of depositing his total salary every month, contained only two thousand dollars!

She couldn't believe it. Once again she had allowed herself to be used. She cried, made herself a cup of tea, and sat down at the kitchen table to put herself through a brutal course of introspection. The first time she had allowed a husband to betray her, she had an excuse: She was very young, naïve enough to believe him, and inexperienced in the ways and possible weaknesses of men. But now, twenty years later, shouldn't she have learned anything? Shouldn't she have been more aware and watchful?

She obviously was an enabler, and men took advantage of her. But now there was more at stake than her pride. She had others to watch out for beside herself. She had the responsibility for her sons. She took stock of her situation. She had a good job and could support them and maintain a home by herself. If she divorced, she would be depriving them of a father. But what kind of father? Did she want her boys to grow up developing his reprehensible values?

They had been married for seventeen years, but this was the end. She made him move out, got a divorce, and is now bringing up her sons alone.

"I'll never again trust men. They justify everything they do and don't do. I am bringing up my sons to be kind, considerate people with a sense of responsibility. I found I had to counteract the dishonest behavior they saw in their father during their every-other-weekend visitations. I used to have to point out his misleading statements to the boys, but as they grew older—they're now twelve and fifteen—they began to see for themselves and I no longer have to point out his corrupt values."

After a while Teresa started dating. The pleasures of total freedom were now palling a bit as she missed male companionship. But as with all the women we interviewed, men were second in need to her children's interests. "I would love to have a relationship with a man as a companion, lover—but he would have no input with my sons. I will not risk any man destroying everything I teach them."

Then a friend introduced her to a nice man who had been divorced and had no children. They began seeing each other regularly. Teresa enjoyed his companionship, the fun of dining out, going to the movies, and having a male in her life. They slept together, but only in his home—she didn't feel her sons were ready for that yet. He got along with the boys although their contact with him was minimal.

Everything was going along well, and she began to waiver in her idea of never having a man move into her home. Then one evening at dinner, she mentioned that her ex was a dismal failure as a father to her sons. He suddenly went silent, and she was puzzled. That was the last she heard from him. Weeks later, she finally called him and asked what happened. He was silent for a moment and then said, "Teresa, I like you, maybe even love you. But I'm uncomfortable with kids, I really don't like them and could never live with them. Your kids obviously need a father figure—well, that can't be me."

Teresa has moved ahead in her career and now holds a responsible and high-paying position. She has no problem managing her finances, owns her house, and has established financial plans for her and her sons' future. She is a vibrant, charming, and attractive woman with an active social life. She is very proud of her boys—and herself. She stated emphatically that she does not see any sort of permanent male/female relationship right now. "Only when my sons are grown and on their own—then, maybe. But marriage—no. I don't want to ever again get tied into marital financial arrangements.

"The first ten years, I gave to my first husband, the next twenty years I gave to my second husband. The rest of my life is mine!"

SHE DID IT HER WAY

THE PURPOSE OF this book is to show women that there are many routes to take in life and that following the conventional paths may not be the best way for you. When you have to make decisions, it seems easiest to do what "They" have always done in such circumstances: Mothers are the best ones to lecture you on what the much-quoted but totally mythical "They" would or would never do.

When you are in extremis about love, relationships, men, and marriage—even when circumstances dictate that you take specific steps that have always been taken in such situations— don't say "yes" when your heart says "no." No one is the best judge of what is right for you than you. It may seem frightening to go into heretofore uncharted territory without the seemingly comforting assurance that others have taken steps being urged on you. It takes courage to go it alone, to do what you know is right for you. But in the long run, you will be happier, feel strong, fulfilled, and have the great satisfaction of never having to say the three saddest words in the English language—"I should have."

Here is the story of a woman who was forced to move from girlhood to womanhood in minutes without letting it become a disaster that could have destroyed her. She gave in, but did not give up. Instead, she built a solid life by learning to believe in herself and developing a strong moral core based on a firm sense of right and wrong. Her two driving concerns were the happiness of her two children and her own need for independence. She succeeded in both by dint of strength and courage, thus proving that women can have it all.

SUZANNE, THE PREGNANT VIRGIN

SHE WAS NINETEEN, Peter had been her boyfriend since she was fifteen, but having sex was something her convent-trained Catholic mother had warned her against forever. "Not until you're married!" So when the doctor told her she was pregnant, she said it was impossible; they never had intercourse, and it was just petting in the backseat. No one had explained the full meaning of sex, the clinical details of genitalia, and the fact that sperm are ferociously active little swimmers that can accomplish their mission—even without penetration. It only takes one, so technically, she was a virgin but actually she was pregnant, a "splash pregnancy."

Her father cried when he heard it because he knew that was the end of her dreamed-of dancing career. Her mother called Peter and told him he had to marry her daughter at once. He was willing, but Suzanne was not. She did not love him, she didn't even know if she really liked him. But she was young, innocent, and obedient. She did what her mother told her. So at age twenty, she got married and had a son.

Thus began a marriage that was devoid of love and affection. Like many men of that era, Peter thought affection was taken care of only in bed. She had come to hate sex, a feeling that took her years to get over. She could not understand his lack of attention. There was none of the sort of caring she had seen in her parents' home. He never complimented her, about her cooking, her appearance, anything. He never seemed to be able to make a living and was always "between jobs." Still, she stayed and had her second son three years later. Finally, she got a legal separation and divorced when she was twenty-eight.

Then she began to start her new life. First, she decided to have her tubes tied. "I had seen second marriages where kids have half-brothers and sisters, and are unhappy because their mom's attention goes to her new babies. Should I ever marry again, I didn't want my boys to have to suffer that."

Untrained, unskilled, she went for the first job available and became a waitress. For the rest of their childhoods, she never used baby-sitters, only leaving them in the care of friends or relatives. "My boys were my life."

As her abilities became apparent, she was promoted and began to build a life for herself. She felt very strongly that she did not need to be taken care of, but wanted to build a solid, happy family home like her parents had—albeit without a father. "I never felt my boys needed a man." However, she did.

First, there was Robert, whom she respected and cared about. They dated for five years, seeing each other a few times a month. He had been married and had custody of his small daughter upon whom he doted, much as she did with her sons. They never even talked about getting married since neither one wanted to be or expose their children to stepparents. After five years, he got involved with training for a new career and left the relationship.

Suzanne began to truly enjoy the single life. She liked the

romance, the wining and dining, the freedom of noncommitted relationships with men. What she valued most was her hard-won independence. Her family developed a tremendous respect for her and admired the life she had made for herself and her children. By now, she was earning enough money to give her sons and herself the style of living she always dreamed of.

Then came Matt. He was a mailman, and they had a pleasant relationship. But she became annoyed at his weakness and attachment to his very domineering mother. "He never took my side or bawled her out when she was rude to me. The last straw was when we went to her house for her birthday. I had made a special lasagna for the occasion, and she wouldn't even bother to come out of her room. When he failed to even try to convince her to join us in the dining room, I figured 'I'm out of here.'"

SHE DECIDED SHE needed time to be by herself. Her sons were now grown and independent. Then along came Donald, a policeman. He had been married three times and was overbearing, but professed his love for her constantly—a flattering change from the nice, soft-spoken ineffectual mailman. He was tough, he was exciting—like no other man she had met before. Like many cops, he kept guns at home and taught her how to shoot.

Since her sons were not around, she was not worried about his macho tactics rubbing off on them. They were together for five years during which he constantly asked her to marry him, but she kept refusing. This was not the kind of man she wanted to spend her life with. The thing that bothered her most was that he had a frightening temper.

After years of renting, Suzanne was able to buy her own condo. One night, Donald arranged to help her move some of her furniture he had kept for her in his garage. When they were loading the furniture into his truck, he said to her with great macho pride and self-assurance, "See—I told you that you need me."

She became infuriated. She had worked for all these years to become totally self-reliant, to need no one but herself, and he was relegating her into the position of the helpless little woman.

"I don't even need you for a ride home!" and she stormed out of his house and started to walk home—two miles a night on the main highway. She expected him to come and get her. But he never did. She used her cell phone to reach her son who came for her. As far as she was concerned, that was the end of Donald. Unfortunately, he did not agree.

One evening, a few weeks later, she heard the doorbell ring. It was Donald asking to please come in. She hesitated, but figured he might want to apologize—so she opened the door. He immediately beat her viciously across the face with the expertise of a professional assailant—using an open hand so that no marks would be visible and all damage would be internal. "You won't marry me, then I'll beat you to death." Finally, he left, and she was shaken, in pain, and horribly frightened. She figured there was no point in reporting his attack to the precinct since no cop would ever record an assault by a fellow cop. But the next day, her friend told her she must report it so that it would be on the record in case he ever tried to hurt her again. So she did.

Then she decided she would never allow herself to be a victim and live in fear. She phoned him and said, "I've reported your violence, so you'd better keep away. I have a gun. Remember you taught me to shoot? I'm warning you—if you ever dare to come anywhere near me, I promise I'll kill you."

It took her a year to get over that horrible experience, and she began to think that no man meant it when he said, "I love you." She thought, men say they love you to get sex, and women use sex to get love.

She enjoyed being alone, but finally decided she was ready for some male companionship. So she checked the "Personals" column—and there was Tom, a lovely man and as usual, the direct opposite of the man she just left. He was gentle, impractical, artistic, unrealistic—a true Flower Child. They dated for four years, but their times together were often made difficult by his young daughter, whose happiness was his primary concern. Suzanne got tired of having the child accompany them to the movies or dinner if she felt like joining them. He had no intention of doing anything to disturb his relationship with his daughter, just as Suzanne felt about herself and her sons. Neither one of them would ever consider remarrying or even having a deep, meaningful relationship.

Suzanne was now fifty-two...attractive, vivacious, self-confident, and self-assured. She had accomplished everything she had aimed for—she had a loving relationship with her sons, who were grown and self-sufficient, she had the respect and admiration of her family, she had developed a career that provided her with a great lifestyle...and she was totally free. She thoroughly enjoyed the singles life. Then she met Charles.

Handsome, suave, he had a laid-back quality that made him highly susceptible to the charms of this spirited, independent woman. He had been divorced for two years, and they started dating. This went on for two years until she realized that she truly loved him and enjoyed his companionship; she was ready to live with him, something she had never felt like before. She proposed the move, but to her surprise, he refused. Living together without benefit of clergy was morally unacceptable to him. Would she marry him? She decided the time was right, the man was right, she was ready. And so they were married.

*Take care! Kingdoms are destroyed by bandits, houses by rats,
and widows by suitors.*
—THE JAPANESE FAMILY STOREHOUSE BY IHARA SAIKAKU, 1683

11

WHY WIDOWS SHOULDN'T MARRY: YOU'VE BEEN THROUGH ENOUGH

THE WORD "WIDOW" carries a past of pain. Whether her husband died shockingly suddenly or agonizingly slowly, a widow has undergone anguish from which, in some sense, she will never totally recover. The experience affects different women in different ways and creates behavioral responses that are often unexpected. One response, however, that every widow can expect almost immediately from friends, acquaintances, and relatives will be a prediction, which is probably meant to be a mix of comfort and flattery. In reality, it is actually insensitive and offensive.

"Mark my words, you'll remarry, and sooner than you think."

It is incredible how normally considerate and kindly people feel that the loss of a woman's husband permits them to enter her bedroom and private life with advice and intimate questions that they would never think of discussing were she married. Tasteless questions about her "love life" and unsolicited guidance on how to proceed with the search for a new mate, which everyone assumes is the goal of every widow, laced with dire warnings about the shortage of eligible men are the common topics of conversation.

Everybody's a maven in the matrimonial marketplace. If she had a good marriage, the popular position will be that she'll want to replicate the situation as fast as possible. If she had a miserable marital relationship, then naturally now she will want to wipe out the disastrous past by making a happy and satisfactory union. In any case, everybody has the reason why she must immediately embark upon a concerted drive to find a new husband.

No one bothers to think about what the widow has begun to think about. Which is—"Why the hell should I ever want to remarry?" Why indeed. Other than completing the couple symmetry of friends' dinner tables, why does she have to be half of a team to be socially acceptable? And if she must take a partner with her on social occasions, why does he have to be a spouse?

Remarriage is no longer the knee-jerk response of widows. Today, there are alternative lifestyles available to women that allow them to evaluate all the elements of reentering matrimony and make judgments based upon personal rather than societal demands.

YOU CAN'T RE-CREATE THE PAST. WHY COMPLICATE YOUR FUTURE?

JOAN'S HUSBAND OF twenty-seven years had a massive coronary on the tennis court in the middle of their regular Sunday morning doubles game. Despite the immediate ministrations of physicians on adjacent courts, he died before reaching the hospital. Although he was overweight, with a gourmand appetite that leaned heavily toward fourteen-ounce steaks and side orders of garlic bread, coupled with working in the high-stress advertising field, he had a perfect health history and literally had never been sick a day in his life.

Joan was an intelligent, capable woman who worked as a psychologist for the local school system, but nothing had prepared her for the sudden loss of the man she had loved and fully expected to live with for at least another twenty to thirty years. Surrounded by her children and friends, she went through all the details and rituals of the funeral with the calm competence everyone expected from her.

Almost immediately thereafter, she sold their house and moved into a nearby apartment. Concerned friends were happy to notice that she was going out and keeping busy and adjusting well to her tragic loss. What no one realized was just how much she was going out and why.

For that first year, Joan went someplace, any place, virtually every evening after work in order to avoid facing the empty apartment. As time passed and she looked back over that period, Joan realized she remembered nothing of the first six months after her husband's death. Although her calm allayed the concerns of friends, her deceptive demeanor was merely a cover-up for the fact that she was in shock.

It took Joan another year to recover and reconcile herself to the fact that her husband was gone and the life she had taken for granted was over. At that point, she began to rebuild her existence and plan for the future. Remarriage was not part of it. What for? There were strong reasons for her marrying twenty-eight years ago, none of which applied now.

Then she was a young girl living at home with her parents, awaiting the arrival of Mr. Right who would carry her off and give her a home, family, security, and a properly married place in society. She had all that now, plus the immense personal satisfaction of a successful career.

What could a husband add to her life at this point except complication, conflict, and compromise? When you live with a man for many years, including those young formative ones when flexibility plus passion make it easier to adapt to each other's wishes, you develop a communion of tastes and attitudes that makes your day-to-day living comfortable and predictable. You know what to expect from each other in almost all situations because you have been through it before. Remarriage at a mature stage in life means adapting to someone whose habits you had no part in formulating, whose reactions to familiar situations will be totally unfamiliar and potentially unpleasant.

Think of all the life experiences, major and minor, that married couples encounter together for the first time to which they form a joint reaction that anneals into permanent attitudes and habits. Maybe it was that first trip to Europe when their introduction to the continental luxury of breakfast in the room developed into their thenceforth automatic hotel routine. Or when they started preparing meals together and found they both hated facing a sink full of pots and dishes after a satisfying meal, which got them into the technique of keeping food warm on the hot tray while a preprandial cleanup was effected.

Everyday life is filled with these little idiosyncrasies that become basic habits and make it more difficult to adapt to living with another person who does not share or even understand them. And the older we get, the more difficult it is to change or compromise.

Cynthia's mother remarried a lovely man who unintentionally terrorized her with complaints about her cooking because she did not use the spices to which he was accustomed. He badgered her until she became almost paralyzed with uncertainty at the stove she had worked over for fifty years. With great difficulty, she finally learned how to prepare food to please him.

Women are used to being the ones called upon to make the compromises. In a *Time* magazine story, "Are Women Fed Up?"

E. James Lieberman, a Washington psychiatrist who specializes in couple's therapy, observed, "Women are still giving more than they get."

In an article in the *New York Times*, Katha Pollitt wrote, "Both sexes have been socialized to see relationship-maintenance as primarily a woman's responsibility....We live in a society that drums into women's heads from the minute they're born that they are here on earth to play supporting roles in essentially male dramas. Marriage has traditionally been one such drama, but so is American culture itself."

If Joan were to remarry, she would have to remake her life over in the image of the man she married. His needs would have to be met, and for many reasons, men seem to have more needs than women. It does not require reading of feminist tracts to become aware of the inflated sense of male entitlement that has been nurtured by families and society. Men are brought up with the implicit expectation of being served by women. Women, on the other hand, have been raised and socialized to be accommodating.

JOAN WAS A woman who did not like to be alone. Or so she thought. She had always enjoyed coming home and getting dinner started in anticipation of her husband's hour-later arrival when they would have drinks and discuss their day's activities. It was a warm, pleasant ritual because it was held against the background of a shared lifetime of interests and concerns. Conversations involved their children, their careers that both had helped each other build, relatives, and familiar family feuds. There was no way Joan could ever expect to duplicate those exchanges with a man with whom she would have only the most recent frames of reference. If she remarried, she might reproduce the situation, but never the elements that gave it value.

Joan opted to not remarry and announced her decision to all who would listen. But no one believed her. It is just another one of those double-standard devilments that beset women forever that a widower's statement of reluctance to remarry is accepted instantly whereas a widow's is viewed as a cover-up for her undesirability. And this skewed reaction does not come from men only.

THE PLEASURES OF THE SINGLE LIFE

RIGHT AFTER DORIS' husband died unexpectedly of a heart attack, her widowed friends rallied around to console and comfort her.

"Give yourself a chance to settle into a single life before you make any big changes. You may not ever want to remarry. We don't."

Doris did not believe them. How could a woman prefer to live without a husband? Although at fifty-three she had a career as a merchandise manager that she had resumed when her two sons were grown, she was very dependent upon her husband for handling the finances and making the major decisions in their lives. She felt lost, lonely, and in limbo without him and assumed all other women felt the same.

"Poor things, they can't find husbands," Doris thought about her widowed friends. "It's just sour grapes when they say they're not looking to get married again."

With the help of her sons, Doris sold her suburban home and bought an apartment in the city near her office and became enthusiastic and excited about her new neighborhood and lifestyle. Many evenings, she walked home from work and thoroughly enjoyed exploring and discovering small tucked-away shops and details of architectural elegance that she had never before noticed.

She found satisfaction in handling the details of her life and began to appreciate the absence of pressures imposed by dependence. No longer did she have to watch the clock nervously and feel the pull to notify her husband that she might be late. If she came across an interesting restaurant on her way home, there was nothing to stop her from having dinner on impulse without having to contend with a balking husband who was never adventurous when it came to food. And when her department required a buying trip to Asia, she did not have to pass up the opportunity because her husband refused to be alone for so long a period. Now she went freely and had a marvelous time.

Doris began to appreciate aloneness. There was a quiet peace in her apartment that she grew to love. She had plenty of activity at her office and interaction with people all day long. She looked forward to her home as a comfortable retreat and respite from the hectic business world. To give her life the structure most of us require, Doris developed a routine and like all widows, began to discover how much of her married life had been devoted to the demands and desires of her husband.

As she created little rituals designed to please only herself, she realized how much of what and when she ate, what she bought, what she wore, what TV programs she watched, even what books she read, had been influenced by her husband's desires and opinions. Even though he was not overbearing, or tyrannical, he managed in his own gentle way to make his likes and dislikes apparent. And being a woman and wife who was trained to please, she had tailored her activities, behavior, and the running of the household to suit him.

Little by little, the liberation process evolved as Doris bought the beautiful wide-brimmed hat that she hadn't permitted herself since the time her husband said she was too short for a big hat and it made her look like a mushroom. Next she broke out into buying clothes in the bright colors she loved, but had eschewed in favor of the subdued tans and grays her husband preferred. She started cooking with abandon, experimenting with new recipes containing the many exotic spices available in her new neighborhood, without fear of incurring disapproval from a husband who preferred simple foods and regarded all dishes that were unfamiliar to be inedible. She bought a subscription to the ballet instead of the once-in-a while performances that she sometimes managed to drag her grumbling spouse to attend.

As Doris exposed herself to more and more new experiences, she realized how much of herself she had subconsciously suppressed over the years in order to make her husband happy and to avoid conflict.

In a longtime marital relationship, each person is changed by the attitudes of the other often to the point of radical transformation. These altering forces frequently work to the partner's benefit as in the cases of those who blossom into confident, attractive individuals with new positive images of themselves derived from the admiration of spouses. Many develop courage to achieve instilled by their mates' supportive belief and encouragement. But more often, the changes effected by the dynamics of living together are less dramatic and result in subtle restraints and behavior modifications that in time become imperceptible because they seem built in. It is only when the strictures are removed that the surviving spouse becomes aware of how much of herself she has sacrificed for peace and a way of life she valued—at the time.

BUT AT THIS point in time, what does marriage offer? Doris was now a different person. She flourished in her new free life and discovered the joys and satisfactions of independence. When she needed advice about financial matters, once handled totally by her husband, she conferred with her sons and made her own decisions, helped but not bound by their suggestions. True, she often missed the loving relationship she had with her husband and felt sad knowing it could never be again. But having sons upon whom she could depend to care for and love her did much to fill the void.

Then she met Lewis, a sixty-year-old widower, who was an accountant in an adjacent office. They started dating casually at first, and soon found they were spending all their leisure time together. Within a few months, it developed into an intimate and relaxed relationship that became important to both of them.

Most weekends he slept at her house, and they took vacation trips together. But when he went home, as he always did, to his apartment, which was about a half-hour's drive from hers, she found she liked his leaving. A year went by, and one of her coworkers asked her when she and Lewis were getting married.

"Married?" said Doris. "But I don't want to get married." And then she saw the questioner's skeptical smile and suddenly thought "My God, she doesn't believe me." She remembered her own incredulity at similar expressions from her widowed friends. But now she knew they were telling the truth, because she would never consider marrying Lewis even though she loved him.

She had come to treasure her independence and freedom and was proud of the highly satisfactory life she had carefully constructed that enabled her to pursue every avenue of interest to her without restriction. She liked to wake up in bed next to Lewis, sometimes. She liked to spend evenings and days with Lewis, sometimes. She liked to be with Lewis because she wanted to be, not because she had to be. She liked when he arrived, and she liked when he left and she could close her door and return to the total privacy of her home. She liked to be free, and she knew she would never, never marry.

When Cynthia's husband died and people, who shouldn't have, asked her if she planned to remarry, the answer was always "never." It's a simple definitive word, but few seemed to understand it. "You mean right now, it's never?" "No," she said, "Always, it's never."

Cynthia was happily married for thirty-five years in an era when marriage was the only socially acceptable lifestyle. The marriage was happy, companionable, and loving replete with all the proverbial ups and downs expected in a long-term relationship. But it ended with the worst possible "down" to be encountered in marriage, the severe, protracted, and ultimately fatal illness of a mate. Which is one big reason why many widows past middle age will not remarry, ever.

THE JOB DESCRIPTION READS "NURSE"

CONSIDER THE POTENTIAL husbands for women in their late forties, fifties, sixties, and older: men in their fifties, sixties, and older who are candidates for heart attacks, strokes, and all the other health disasters that occur with alarming frequency in men of these ages. When you marry young and years later your husband becomes ill and/or incapacitated, you love him and care for him willingly. You married for better or worse, and this is the worse. It is the fair and equitable price for the many years of health and happiness that you shared. But to marry a fifty-or-over man who is just entering the high-risk health years is courting disaster, and the job description reads "nurse."

Twice when Cynthia attended funerals of men who had died unexpectedly, she found herself in the sobbing arms of their grieving wives who said through tears, "At least you were able to be prepared when David died. For me, it's such a horrible shock."

Cynthia forgave them for the imbecility of their statements and wrote it off to the unbalancing effect of bereavement. They were, in effect, telling her how lucky she was to have lived with six years of illness and deterioration to ready herself for the ultimate end. Cynthia would have liked to tell them that no matter how often you face the possibility of an ill loved one's death, nothing in the world can prepare you for the utter desolation of defeat over losing a long-fought battle or for the numbing sense of finality of the death itself.

Unless you have lived through the anguish of watching a person you love undergo pain, agony, fear, and disintegration, you cannot possibly comprehend the utter despair and hopelessness that pervades every waking moment of your life. When you see an elderly woman in an airport, restaurant, or museum pushing a wheelchaired husband, your heart should go out to her because Herculean efforts have gone into this public presentation of normalcy; the washing, wiping, cleaning up urine and feces, dressing and feeding that was preparatory to this trip and are her twenty-four-hour responsibility. Few women who have undergone the wrenching experience of caring for a dying spouse will be eager to remarry and risk a repeat of this ordeal.

The high-rise buildings that line the main avenues of southern Florida are filled with white-haired widows who are active, involved, and happy. They go to dances, which are very popular in Florida, designed to imitate the social functions of their youth and also to afford them chances to show off the mambo and samba lessons that cost them a small fortune. They go to meet men whom they want to date and dance with, but not marry.

As one widow said, "You see that guy sitting in the corner? He's not dancing because he just had a bypass. That one on the dance floor is OK now that he got his new pacemaker. They want to get married, I hear. A woman would be crazy to marry them. They're not looking for wives, they're looking for nurses!"

Men of that age and condition cannot live alone, so they seek wives to cook for them, care for them, and listen to their complaining, which is a big part of such relationships. Menstrual cramps inure women to pain from an early age, and they grow up with an almost stoic ability to deal with hurt and discomfort. Men seem to be in constant need of sympathy, and the more advanced in age they are, the more advanced their ailments and requisite demands for succor. Who needs it?

Most of these elderly widows have become savvy enough to realize the drawbacks of remarriage. Every widow interviewed reiterated the relative contentment of living without the compromises required by a husband. Here are just some of their comments:

"I have a wonderful busy life."

"I enjoy my privacy."

"I don't have to give in to anyone else. I do what I want."

"I can eat a grilled cheese at eleven o'clock if I feel like it and not have to shop and cook a big dinner."

"I found that there's life after men."

"What good are men? They don't have the same interests as women do. They never talk. Women always seem to dredge up something to talk about. You can sit at dinner with a man and not exchange a single word for an hour—unless you start up a conversation."

"I do fine handling my own life. I don't need any help."

"Who needs to wash another man's socks?"

"Who wants those old men? Do you know one date I had told me he couldn't get an erection, and he wanted me to help? The nerve of him, I hardly knew the man, and he wants me to go to bed with him and work yet."

Unfortunately, some widows get sucked into the old sales pitch that a woman needs a husband to take care of her and that an unmarried woman is automatically banished into social exile. Bewildered by their new widowhood, afraid of the unknown, they are panicked into remarriage too quickly without allowing themselves the time to become acquainted with themselves and their abilities to live alone and like it.

THE DANGERS OF A RUSHED REMARRIAGE

DEBBY'S HUSBAND OF forty-two years died after a long bout with cancer. She was weary, dispirited, and grief stricken. At sixty-seven years old, she felt like eighty. Emerging from many years of being a wife, she had in essence lost her "job" and now perceived herself as being worthless. What would she do for the rest of her life?

A few months after her husband's death, she ran into Warren, an old friend who had moved away years earlier and had recently returned to the area. His wife had just died, also of cancer. Their common experience created a new empathy between them, and they began to see each other regularly.

After just three months, he asked her to marry him. She was stunned and totally unprepared. She had just about completed all the myriad of details and assorted legalities that ensue after death, like changing listings, redeeming insurance policies, and sundry assorted minutiae that must be handled by the surviving spouse. She had not yet had the time to start building a life on her own. She was uncomfortable, it all seemed too soon. Neither she nor Warren was concerned about the propriety of remarriage so shortly after their mates' demises since the protracted dying period eliminated the need for extended mourning. But Debby was in a dilemma over how to respond to Warren's proposal.

Debby was uncertain and totally lacking in the confidence to make any major decisions. Her inadequacy made her the perfect prey of not-always-well-meaning friends and relatives who claim to know what's best for everyone. They pointed out what a great catch and once-in-a-lifetime opportunity this marriage offered. ("You're not a youngster, you know. How many more chances will you get? If you don't grab him, there's a line of women who will. A good-looking, well-to-do man like him can have his pick of younger women. You're lucky you caught him before he got out into the market.")

Debby liked Warren, but did not love him. She found him pleasant and easy to be with. Perhaps practicality should outweigh passion at this time in life, right? Her husband just died, his wife just died, it seemed fortuitous...maybe even fated. So Debby said, "Yes."

The first stabs of disquiet came at the lawyer's office where they all met to sign the prenuptial agreement. Her children pointed out that their father's money should eventually rightfully be theirs, and the only way to ensure this was with an agreement. This seemed logical to Debby. The trouble came when she encountered the grasping hostility of Warren's three daughters who obviously regarded their father's new marriage as a plot to deprive them of their birthright. Warren tried to assuage their fears, and after everybody had been fully assured by the attorneys that Debby's children would be her sole heirs and Warren's children would be his, the papers were signed. They quickly married, and Debby moved into Warren's house since it was more luxurious and larger than hers.

It was strange for Debby to be living in another woman's house. She missed her small, but familiar home, which she had already rented to a French family who signed a two-year lease. Warren's house was nice, but it wasn't hers, and when she expressed her discomfort, he insisted that she refurnish the house to suit her tastes.

The project started out as fun, and Warren even joined her in the shopping. They started to enjoy selecting and discussing new pieces and color schemes. Then the daughters heard and came screaming. "How dare you throw out my mother's furniture and drapes? It's all in perfectly good condition."

They accused Debby of senseless extravagance and told their father he had married a selfish woman who was trying to waste his money and should be controlled.

Debby was shocked. A rather shy, sensitive person, she did not know how to cope with such crude behavior and active hostility. She turned to Warren, expecting him to admonish his daughters for their insulting assault on his wife and was stunned at his silence. He did not defend her. He did not explain that he had suggested the refurnishing. He did not chastise them for their reprehensible display of disrespect for an older woman. He did not warn them that attacks upon his wife would not be tolerated. He just sat there.

"What have I gotten into?" thought Debby in despair. "What kind of man is this? What kind of family is this that I am now part of?"

When she discussed his daughters' behavior with Warren after they had stormed out of the house, he was sheepish, but not apologetic. In fact, he thought that she was overreacting, because he assumed all mothers and daughters screamed at each other. He was surprised to hear that Debby's relationship with her daughter was calm and pleasant, and even though arguments occurred, insulting rudeness was unacceptable. He told her to disregard his daughters' behavior "They were just upset. They didn't mean half of what they said." Those kinds of battles were commonplace between his former wife and the girls, and they all got over it in no time. Debby pointed out that whereas his wife was their mother, she was not, and emotional upheavals that take place between parents and children are totally different from those that occur with strangers.

"Oh, you're making too much of this, Debby," he said cajolingly. "Why don't we just forget the whole thing?"

But Debby could not, especially since his daughters made it their business to drop in constantly and made her feel that she was under active surveillance. They were sullen and ungracious and scanned the house constantly looking for additions or subtractions to the furnishings. There was an extremely unpleasant episode when one of the daughters spotted the unfamiliar silk bedspread in the master bedroom.

"How much did that fancy thing cost?" she demanded rudely. Debby looked at her quietly and answered, "I really don't remember. I bought it six years ago."

The daughter did not apologize. Although Warren encouraged Debby to go ahead with her refurnishing plans, she lost heart and found the entire matter too distasteful. The prospect of having to defend her purchases to those harridans was not worth the acquisitions. Their constant remarks about the stupidity of buying new things, when you're so old and the ridiculous amortization ratio of spending $1,000 for something that you'll barely live long enough to enjoy, were offensive and aggravating.

What was worse, however, was Warren's total inability to understand her resentment of his daughters' treatment of her. "Just don't listen. Ignore them," he said. But she couldn't. Her whole life became polluted by the acrimony engendered by Warren's family.

They resented her, they disliked her, and they vented their feelings continually.

Warren was a nice man and comparatively undemanding. She enjoyed his company and could have adjusted to serving dinners he liked and arranging his clean laundry in his drawers the way he preferred.

Having recently left one position as wife and housekeeper, it was simple to adapt to the new job. She was accustomed to serving and subordinating her wishes to those of a man. But she could not countenance the disruptive behavior of the daughters nor what she considered her husband's lack of respect for her.

Then the day came when Warren announced that his daughters had persuaded him to set up a trust whereby all his money would be held in a trust fund that his daughters would manage. He explained that this was merely a device to avoid future inheritance taxes and would alter nothing in their present lives.

When Debby mentioned this to her son who was a trust-and-estates attorney, he told her that Warren's ability to spend money would now be monitored by his children. She was horrified to realize that these hostile women would now have a say over whatever she bought and would in effect take control of her life. Her son noticed how upset she became and wanted to know why.

Up to that point, she had never mentioned her unhappiness to her children, feeling that this was her problem and she would handle it. As far as they knew, her marriage was fine. When her son heard the entire story that she poured out tearfully, he was infuriated. He wanted to confront Warren immediately, but she pleaded with him to hold off until she had a chance to think things through and determine what action she wished to take.

The next morning over breakfast, Debby broached the subject with Warren and explained how difficult she would find living under the financial thumbs of his children. He became so upset that Debby feared he would make himself ill. She realized that although he presented a secure, masterful image, Warren was actually a weak, passive man who had always taken the path of least resistance, which in this instance was to yield to his daughters' demands.

Unlike most men who abhor scenes and are fiercely uncomfortable with overt female displays of emotion, Warren totally ignored them. He had grown up in a house full of women, his father died when Warren was a small child, and he was brought up by his mother and grandmother. His married life was merely a continuation of a female household, only this time it was a wife and daughters. Early on, he had developed his own technique for living with women that consisted of being gentle, charming, and helpless so that they adored him and turned themselves inside out to please him. He always walked away from their attacks, assiduously avoided confrontations, confident that their ire would pass, and their long habit of looking after him would result in a happy ending. Debby was asking him to argue with his daughters, to take an assertive position that he never had assumed before. The concept was unthinkable.

Sorrowfully, she realized that she could not change the habits of a lifetime and that he would never fight for himself, let alone for her. She knew that the only way her marriage would survive was to do what women have done for centuries—give in to her husband's needs. When she told her children of her decision to accept the terms of her marriage, they were upset. Especially her daughter.

"Mother, you have never even given yourself a chance to live alone and find out who you are and what you like. I saw you all my life doing for dad, living the life he wanted, and taking care of him. Now you're in another situation where again you're the caretaker and compromising to please a man. Leave him and his horrible daughters. You don't need his financial support. Go back to your house, and start a new life. Find out what it's like to please only you, to do whatever you want, and not have to consider anyone else. Take the chance. You'll see, you'll love it."

Debby's son listened to his sister's impassioned plea, looked at his uncertain, frightened, close-to-tears mother, and said quietly, "But suppose she doesn't love it?"

Debby's eyes met her son's and she turned to her daughter and said: "No, I have to stay. I'll live with it."

She explained that the known difficulties she would now have to face were preferable to the unknown difficulties she would encounter in the totally unfamiliar life as a single woman. She had always lived this way, and she was used to it. The idea of the terrible daughters doling out money was preferable to the fears she had of handling her own finances. Living with a man for whom she had lost all respect was still better than living with no man at all.

So she stayed and faced the once-a-month criticism about her excessive number of long-distance phone calls, questions about the need to have her hair and nails done every week, lifted eyebrows when she wore a new dress or pair of shoes. She hated the garish foil wallpaper in the bathroom and den, but knew that there was no possibility of alteration. And worst of all, she lived with a man who cared more for his own comfort and peace of mind than he did for her, whom she could never trust because in the last analysis, he was her husband, but not her friend.

THE FEAR OF FINANCIAL MANAGEMENT

DEBBY WAS LIKE a prisoner who is released after forty-two years and becomes a recidivist because of a now ingrained inability to cope with the complications and demands of freedom. All widows who have lived sheltered lives where the husbands took full charge of finances, bill paying, car maintenance, and taking out the garbage are frightened at first, and the older they are, the more scared they are. At first, they recoil from the strange-looking bills and statements that seem so forbidding. They marvel at the brilliance and capability of their husbands who were able to deal with all those complicated-looking papers. They become confused and angry and look for someone else, like a child or grandchild, to take charge of all these onerous details.

All they need is for someone to sit down with them, force them to confront the details, and show how easy it is to pay a bill and record payment, whether it be for a charge account, insurance premium, mortgage, or rent. They start tentatively and then, surprised at the simplicity, get into more depth and eventually take tremendous pride in their ability to run their own affairs. You know they're OK when you hear, "Huh, what's the big deal? Here I thought Sam was such a genius. Write a few checks, make a few notes, that's all there is to it."

One woman admired her husband extravagantly for what she thought was his intense business acumen because he had accounts in seven banks. After he died, and she was subjected to the nuisance of visiting seven banks to transfer funds, she realized that he kept a few thousand dollars in each merely to be able to boast every time they traveled through the city, "You see that bank? We have money in there." Her financial idol quickly developed clay feet, and in no time, she was handling her own bills and banking.

Once the money mystique, perpetuated by husbands who want to enslave wives into dependency, is exposed in all its actual simplicity, widows get down to the business of building lives of proud independence. When they finally have control of their own financial positions and futures—why should they even consider marrying again?

If Debby had not had the misfortune of being presented with an opportunity for remarriage so quickly after she became widowed, she would have been forced to face up to her imagined inadequacy. She would have gotten over the first fright of solitude and learned to balance a checkbook, hire a contractor, buy her own car, and deal with the details of running her own life. She could have developed a self-esteem that would never permit the kind of abuse she was now willing to accept from her husband and his family. But Debby was a victim of her time and was one of the unquestioning believers of the myth that a woman must marry in order to be a whole person. A definition of the word "myth" in the American Heritage Dictionary of the English Language states: "A notion based more on tradition or convenience than on fact." Just so—but whose convenience? Why, men's, of course.

I would be married, but I'd have no wife,
I would be married to a single life.
—Richard Crashaw

12

THE "CLOSET SINGLES"

THEY ARE ATTRACTIVE, charming women who claim to want husbands, but never seem to be able to find the right one. Of course not, because it's not men they find wanting—it's marriage. How many times have you heard people say, "She's a good-looking woman—I wonder why she never found a husband?"

There is always the assumption that marriage is every woman's goal, and divergence from the pattern is puzzling. If she had never been married, well then she just wasn't the sort men found desirable, but if she proved her bride-ability, there seems to be no rational reason why she hasn't found another husband. It's not because she has not been looking. Over the years, she has gone out with a succession of men and continues to reiterate that she wants to get married. But as "They" used to put it, "She can't get anyone to take her to the altar."

Did it ever dawn on them, both the social commentators and the women themselves, that they do not want to get married?

These women are "Closet Singles" who have built highly satisfactory lives for themselves and are reluctant to rearrange their homes and activities and priorities to adapt to the needs of men. Some did that already, and it wasn't worth it. The truth is they do not want to be wives. Maybe they never did. They lead busy, fulfilling lives with the privileges of glorious freedom that married women often envy. They never have to cope with a man's demands. They never have to clean up another person's messes. They never have to deal with any neuroses and needs except their own. They never have to mold their mentalities to conform to the compromises required to live happily with husbands. They are single, and they love it.

Unfortunately, society has not allowed them to admit to this heretical fact either to the world at large or even to themselves. So they profess to want wedding bands to prove that someone wants them and yet continue to feel disquietingly different.

WORLDLY, BUT "WEDDED"

MADELINE, AN ENGLISHWOMAN, is now in her seventies and still wears the wedding band from a marriage that took place fifty years ago and lasted one year before she divorced a husband who consummated the marriage on their wedding night and then gave up the disgusting habit at once. The lump-sum settlement her lawyer wisely advised her to accept and invest has kept her comfortable all these years.

Madeline still lives in the house that she came to as a bride and has filled it with memorabilia of her life and elegant souvenirs of her travels. A woman of impeccable taste, she has furnished the house with the carefully chosen antiques accumulated with the eyes and skill of an expert that she has become. What began as an interest developed into a hobby and then a profession as Madeline discovered she had an innate artistry that led to her becoming a writer and lecturer on art and antiques. Every corner of her house shows the talents of the owner and is obviously lovingly cared for with pride and pleasure.

Everybody has tried to "fix her up" with someone. Over the years, she has had a succession of lovers and wild romantic affairs that were the despair and envy of her sister and friends.

"Why don't you pick someone marriageable for once?" they would cry as she trotted out another of the charming, but elusive rogues who would do deliriously unpredictable things like carrying her off to the Riviera on a whim or see to it that she had a roomful of roses when she arrived at a hotel on one of her many trips everywhere.

"He said he plans to divorce his wife," she would explain to everyone. "She doesn't understand him, and he's very unhappy but there are the children . . ."

She was rarely without a man. There was always someone who was dancing attendance and even some who were allowed to move in—for a while. Like the charming Frenchman who was there to have an eye operation and wore a dashing eye patch during his period of convalescence in her home. She was very skilled at attracting men and adept at keeping them as long as she wanted. When the dashing Frenchman started to flirt with the wife of a couple who had been invited to drinks and dinner, the guests found themselves on the street after cocktails with the husband accusing his wife of misunderstanding the invitation.

Her dresser drawers were always filled with the sort of stunning, salacious underwear and nightgowns that married women stare at in windows and wonder who wears them.

She continued to bemoan the marital unsuitability of all the men she seemed to meet, yet she never chose anyone who wasn't.

She did not need financial support so fiscal standing was never a criterion. But stability and the desire to settle down were traits she should have sought if she really wanted to marry.

Madeline claimed that she loved children and wanted to be a mother. But her two nieces seemed to fulfill her maternal instinct yet not interfere seriously with her life. They adored her. She was so much more fun than their serious and disciplined mother and was always involved in interesting activities. They loved her and gave her the comfort of knowing that someone would always be there when needed. Her sister provided the same security in Madeline's life and also the role of the stern, disapproving guardian who watched over her best interests at all times.

Madeline was six years younger than her sister, whom she always regarded as their father's favorite. Like many siblings, each child had a totally different view of their family life. Her sister saw their upbringing as satisfactory, normal, and happy, whereas Madeline remembered only a father who disapproved of her frivolity and disparaged her creativity. Her mother she saw as a sensitive and loving woman who suffered the bullying of an arrogant tyrannical husband. Both daughters dutifully married sons of approved families, but whereas her sister was content to live with a boring man in a totally predictable existence that replicated that of generations of women before her, Madeline wanted more.

A product of her time and upbringing, she would have stayed in the dull, restrictive marriage and never taken the revolutionary step of divorce had not her husband committed the sin that was abhorred by even the most conventional, traditional families—he failed to perform the basic male marital obligation of providing his wife with children and not because he was sterile, but because he was sexually neuter.

In her virginal innocence, Madeline had no way of knowing during the first year of her marriage that her husband's lack of ardor was unusual and the fact that he desired sexual intercourse only three times during the entire twelve months was not normal behavior for a twenty-five-year-old man. Then one Sunday, they were in their parents' kitchen doing the dishes together after a family dinner, and her sister asked why she was not yet pregnant. When Madeline mentioned her infrequency of procreative activity, her sister reacted with shock, and for the first time, Madeline realized something was wrong.

Her sister advised their parents immediately, and Madeline's incensed father arranged a family meeting with the miscreant groom's parents who were totally unmoved and unimpressed by the accusation that their son was not properly performing his marital obligations. Their reaction plus the fact that they had but the one child made Madeline's father deduce that the sluggish sex drive may have been hereditary.

"I don't see what's so terrible," said the mother of the groom. "He's still a good husband and provider, and at least, she'll never have to worry about him running around with other women."

Although her father had always regarded divorce as unmentionable and unthinkable, he felt it was righteous and appropriate under the circumstances and arranged the entire matter. Together with a wise solicitor, they saw to it that Madeline was well compensated for the indignity she had undergone. Her husband had despoiled and disappointed her and forced her into the ignominious role of divorcee, a shameful epithet in those days, and thus must pay her well for his misdeed.

Madeline usually rebelled against her father's orders, but this time she accepted unhesitatingly and gratefully. In truth, she was relieved to be rid of the husband whom she found totally uninspiring and a life she found stultifying. She found herself in the pleasant position of being the pathetic, wronged woman and was treated sympathetically and almost tenderly by her father for the first time in her life.

Everyone felt sorry for her and wanted to help re-establish her life and of course, find another husband. She was invited to endless dinner parties to meet eligible males and found herself enjoying a freedom and sense of abandon she had never experienced before. Since she was now a married woman, she was allowed to live in her own apartment and not reside with her parents as did all proper single girls.

She had a lovely home all to herself with no oppressive father or husband to impose demands and a frantically busy social life that had her out most nights of the week. She was pretty, she was intelligent, and she was free. She loved it, but still mindful of the conditioning that unmarried means unwanted, she wore the wedding ring that branded her Mrs. forever. And she embarked on a life that would have been totally satisfactory had she not been burdened with that emotional baggage of feeling that unmarried is unnatural.

Madeline knew plenty of married couples. By and large, she saw little she coveted. Though she professed to envy her sister's constant access to an escort and secure connubial life, she considered her brother-in-law a crashing bore and the idea of living with such a man to be a punishment. She regarded all the men she knew and had ever known as nice to visit, but she wouldn't want to live with them.

Madeline is a "Closet Single." She never wanted to be married, but she cannot admit the fact even to herself. How much happier she would have been were she a product of now and not then. Today, it is easier for women to decide to not marry, because they have more resources and recourses. Years ago, the "single-minded" woman who was conventional and not courageous plowed ahead into miserable matrimony and was only freed by fate.

DIVORCE: THE FREEDOM FACTOR

BETTY WAS A spunky, bubbly redhead of nineteen when she caught the eye of a thirty-two-year-old bookstore owner in her town who fell madly in love with her and proposed within one month after their meeting. In her very small town, an offer of marriage from a respectable, responsible businessman was considered a coup for any young girl.

Betty was infatuated with John, and her friends thought she was the luckiest girl in the world because he was so intelligent and nice looking even though his hair was starting to thin a bit on top. Betty thought about not having to live in a one-room apartment with a young callow husband who was not yet established. John had a large, sunny, five-room apartment over the store, and it was rumored that he owned the building. They could even afford to have a baby right away if she wanted instead of having to wait a few years until they had built up a bank account.

Of course, Betty's parents approved heartily of the match and considered themselves fortunate that this serious, prosperous man would take charge of their very attractive daughter whose popularity with the boys had always caused problems of discipline and control at home. The wedding was an elaborate affair after which they honeymooned in Bermuda and returned to settle into a life of domesticity and, Betty assumed, automatic bliss.

At first, it was a novelty. But soon Betty began to miss everything and everyone. Married life involved a good deal of drudgery and not too much fun. Betty was a gregarious, energetic woman who enjoyed exploring new situations and new people. John preferred to sit quietly and read on the evenings he was home since the store kept him busy six days and three nights a week. Betty, acting the role of the dutiful wife, adjusted her preferences to suit his, and they lived a sedate and uneventful existence.

Once the awe of her husband subsided, Betty realized that they had little in common, and in fact, she found him unexciting and unappealing. She mentioned her discontent to her mother, who assured her that she would feel differently if she became pregnant because having a child keeps a woman busy and fulfilled.

They had a son the following year, and Betty became even more unhappy. She loved the baby and was a good mother, but caring for an infant involved twenty-four hours of slavery that left her exhausted. Fatigue gave her a good reason to refuse the sexual demands of her husband, which she found tiresome and totally unsatisfying and made her wonder what was the big deal people made about sex. Since she had to be up at night with the baby and John needed his rest in order to be alert the next day for work, Betty persuaded him that for the time being, it would be best if he slept in the spare bedroom while she kept the infant in the room with her.

By the time the baby was a year old, their life had solidified into separate bedrooms, and neither made an effort to change the arrangements, which was fine with Betty. John's business had grown, and there were now three stores that kept him away almost every evening and often weeks at a time when he had to make buying trips or attend conventions.

Six years passed, and their son was in school, leaving Betty somewhat free for the first time in years. She began taking courses to resume the education she had abandoned when she married. She loved the work, she loved the interaction with other students, she loved just getting out of the house and doing something of value.

Then one day, needing stamps to mail off a school paper to her professor and knowing that her husband kept some in his briefcase, she opened the case and found stamps, but also photographs of John and a woman in various stages of undress. Her initial reaction was shock and anger. Her second thought was to hire a detective, who followed her husband long enough to catch him and the other woman in bed in a hotel room thereby supplying the legal evidence required in that state for a divorce.

Armed with alimony from a guilty spouse, Betty moved to the big city, placed her son in a good boarding school, and for the first time in her life, found herself totally free. She got her degree and then went to work for an international charitable organization. Today, she travels all over the world and has just broken up with her latest lover.

During the interim years, she had many dates and relationships always with the stated intention that she wanted to find a good husband. Yet when a man's interest became too intense and the possibility of marriage became imminent, Betty found a reason to cut things off. Everyone wanted to match her up with some man or other, but it never seemed to work out.

"I can't understand it," friends continued to comment. "She's so pretty and has such a marvelous personality. You'd think she'd find a husband in a minute."

She would have—if she wanted one. But deep down, Betty rejects marriage because she prefers to live her own life alone. Her son is now grown, married, and lives in another state, and they have a fine relationship. She has everything she wants when and where she wants it—so why should she marry? She tried it and found she likes single better. Now if she could only admit this to her friends and to herself, she would be happily free of that burden of guilt borne by all women who feel that they are in some way inferior if they do not have proof of ownership of a man—marriage.

FAMILY TIES

FAMILY IS ONE of the most basic elements in all societies. It gives us a structure and sense of belonging that enriches and often controls our existence. As we become adults, we still maintain our love for parents and siblings with whom we grew up, but now our focus is on making our own homes and lives. That's how it should be—but isn't always. The "Dear Abby" columns constantly print letters from unhappy people who claim their spouses never take their sides in disagreements with overbearing in-laws and isn't it time they severed the apron strings? The inevitable answer is "yes," but there's never a surefire suggestion as to how to overcome unusual and often unnatural ties to parents and siblings other than to go for counseling. Sometimes, circumstances have created a pull that is so powerful that it can prevent marriages or break them up, and no amount of self-awareness can effect a cure.

THE SELF-MADE MATRIARCH

KRISTA WAS THE eldest of six children who grew up in Brazil where their father was an executive with an international company. They lived in a community of American families where it was impossible to make long-lasting friends since children came and went as their fathers were transferred. As a result, Krista and her brothers and sisters developed a strong bond since family was the only constant in their lives.

Krista was eighteen when they moved back to the United States permanently, and she went off to college and then graduate school. She got a job with a business-consulting company and was sent all over the world until she decided to settle down in New York City where all her younger siblings already lived. Her father retired, and her parents moved to Florida.

KRISTA HAD MANY friends and an active social life that included a string of relationships, most often with married men. Finally, she met Richard, with whom she developed an intimacy and friendship that involved calling each other numerous times a day and seeing each other a few times a week. Richard had his own public-relations business and had never been married—and one day he said to Krista, "Let's get married." This was a situation she had not encountered, since her married boyfriends had no intention of leaving their wives, and thus Krista never had to think about whether she wanted to marry. Krista could not give Richard an answer. She kept hedging without being able to give him, or herself, a reason.

Then she got a panicked call from her mother saying that her father was hospitalized with a heart attack, and her brother, Keith, had come home to recuperate from a kidney operation. Her mother, who had never been a strong woman and had left the upbringing of her youngest children to Krista, was overwhelmed.

Krista took a leave of absence from her job and flew to Florida, and took over the household, the familiar role she had during her growing-up years. Richard called her every day, and she repeatedly told him she couldn't return to New York and marry him until her family was straightened out. Keith was still ill when her sister, Roseanne, an advertising copywriter, lost her job, could no longer afford her New York apartment, and moved back home.

The months moved on, and Krista was busy taking her father for rehab therapy, administering medications to both Keith and her father. She fell into the familiar role of running the household, paying the bills, driving her mother to the market. As always, everyone turned to her for decisions.

Richard flew down to visit a few times, but was unable to pry her loose from her family. Then two other brothers came home to stay for a few weeks to straighten out problems with work and relationships. Home was, by habit, where all the siblings came when they encountered any difficulties. Not one of the six children ever married. Richard finally gave up, realizing that Krista would never leave her family to create a new one with him. She was the head of the only home she ever wanted.

THE "LOOKING FOR MR. PERFECT" EXCUSE

SHE'S ATTRACTIVE, SHE has lovers and talks constantly of her desire to marry—when the right man comes along. That's a never-married "Closet Single."

Roberta, the pretty, well-groomed forty-ish grade-school teacher, immediately announced that she was not a suitable subject for this book since she has always wanted to get married.

"Then why didn't you?" she was asked.

Her face registered surprise mixed with pleasure. It was probably the first time in twenty years that anyone had made the assumption that her single state was due to her choice. She proceeded to prove the point by telling "horror" stories of the dozens of flawed men she has had the misfortune to encounter since puberty. Each one had some disgusting drawback or character defect that soon became apparent as their friendship developed. No matter how great a man looked at the inception of their relationship, her glorious expectations of perfection were inevitably shattered as familiarity lowered the behavior barriers and he proved himself to be merely human and therefore unacceptable.

She was emphatic, each time she met a new man, she embarked on the friendship with an open heart and mind, filled with the romantic expectation that here at last was the husband of her dreams who would treat her with adoration and consideration and make her "feel good about herself" (a modern term of nauseating narcissism). And each time she had to suffer her mother's constant "so when?" phone calls replete with discussions about the potential wedding guest list.

But alas, when the courtship period passed and the relationship evolved into normal give-and-take, Roberta became disenchanted and refused to take what she saw as the little he was able to give, thereby proving himself to be another man unworthy of the position as her husband.

When asked for specific examples of ways in which this succession of swains had failed, she cited a litany of complaints similar to those heard when a group of wives get together for lunch where the prime topic is usually husband bashing. "He never talks, he never listens, he never appreciates, he forgets, he never understands." (Have you ever noticed that whereas men criticize what women do, women criticize what men do not do?)

What she and other "Closet Singles" view as unforgivable and unendurable, married women find to be irritants, annoyances, and manifestations of male weaknesses. They are willing to accept these flaws because they obviously find the quid pro quo worth the compromise.

Why should she have to compromise if she prefers a free life unfettered by connubial demands? Instead of facing the fact that she truly does not want to marry, she persists in the search for "The Perfect Man," laying out a job description that sounds like a composite of Brad Pitt and Donald Trump.

This woman cannot simply relax and enjoy the pleasures of her chosen single life. Instead, she tortures herself with the eternal quest. She could be comfortable and happy with her lifestyle if she did not pollute her pleasure with a sense of failure that makes her feel unworthy and unwanted and ultimately destroys the possibility of her ever having a happy male-female relationship, married or unmarried.

The "Closet Single" is a woman who frequently has a perennial "boyfriend," a man who has been hanging around like a puppy for years and would marry her like a shot, but whose attentions she alternately scorns, takes advantage of, and takes for granted. But this man's very availability makes him unappealing and knocks him out of the running for the role of Her Husband.

There will never be a "Mr. Right" because she doesn't want to be Mrs. Right but doesn't have the courage to face that fact. She is a "Closet Single" and will only be happy when she stops listening to any voices other than her own.

"Closet Singles" perpetuate their own misery by their inability and/or unwillingness to confront the realization that, for whatever reasons, they truly do not want to be married. Frequently, being conventional women, they shrink at admitting to heterodoxy that would brand them with the dread word "different." They whine about the injustice of Fate that has deprived them of a husband and continue to pursue a lifestyle that precludes all possibilities of acquiring one.

THE MARRIAGE-PREVENTION LIFESTYLE

"HOW DID I get to be forty and not married?" Cora cried last year. A self-supporting freelance copywriter, she had been contentedly living with Ralph for fifteen years when suddenly she decided she should get married because everyone else seemed to be. Their life together quickly deteriorated into anger, accusations, and decisions to leave him, then stay with him and an up-and-down existence that began to drive them both crazy.

When they met, Cora was a pretty, happy twenty-five-year old with vague ideas of settling down someday, but not quite yet. Ralph was a free-spirit type who made his living refinishing furniture, punctuated with winter trips to the Caribbean and the Florida Keys where he worked for scuba-diving schools. He was romantic and adoring, and she loved him and/or the life (she was never sure which). Cora quit her job and traveled with Ralph picking up work wherever they stopped for the winter.

They never mentioned marriage because the concept of home and family never entered the picture. As the years went on, they decided to settle in one place and rented a small house in the suburbs where he opened his own furniture-refinishing business. When she hit forty, Cora began to think she ought to have a home and children, but with whom? She had never viewed Ralph as a husband and father. He was just the man she ate with, had sex with, and shared a house with, but he did not fit the image she had of the Protector Man of the House like her father.

She began to observe married couples, looking for signs of closeness, caring, and respect that she had never built into her relationship with Ralph because they both wanted an independence and individuality that discouraged the collaborative efforts required of marriage. Every aspect of Cora's life was constructed to carefully avoid responsibility of any kind. She would not take a full-time job although she could earn double what she did as a freelancer and have the security of medical and pension benefits. Her refusal was not based on laziness or fear of work; there were many weeks when she put in weekends and nine and ten hours a day. Rather, she needed to know that she could be free whenever she chose and preferred to work on her own terms.

This is just how she wanted everything...on her own terms. Now suddenly she wanted "The American Dream," the whole enchilada...husband, house, kids. Most people seem to be married and happy. Her sister and brother were married. Why wasn't she? Their conventional lives that she had always viewed as banal and dreary now became the ideal state of being. Cora began to reevaluate Ralph, no longer seeing him as the pleasant man she liked coming home to, but as an infuriatingly unaffiliated guy who acted nothing like the husbands she had met. She wanted a baby, but how could she possibly consider unreliable Ralph as a father?

Ralph found himself living with a carping nag who demanded attention, visible displays of affection, manifestations of caring, and constant revelation of his feelings about her, his work, and the world. He was puzzled and confused, and hated to see her so unhappy. Every other day, there was some confrontation about his failure to perform as Cora now wanted.

"We don't communicate!" she would shriek. "Talk to me, for God's sakes!" Mystified and miserable, Ralph was unable to please her. They lived by rules of privacy and independence that had been mutually established years ago but that were now apparently unacceptable to Cora. "Do you want to get married?" he continued to ask, and she continued to refuse because she had an idealized image of marriage that was as flesh and blood as the bride and groom on a wedding cake. There was no way Ralph (or any man) could fit the picture. In reality, their relationship was a good one and in many ways, indistinguishable from many perfectly successful marriages. But that was not the issue.

If Cora truly wanted to be a wife and mother, she would have either married Ralph or moved out and sought a new relationship. But she did neither because she did not want to give up the freedom of being single that allowed her to do whatever she wanted and to take off whenever she wanted.

She really enjoyed her life with Ralph, and their living arrangements had always pleased her enormously—until she reached forty and the old spinster conditioning hit her like a ton of bricks. Then she wanted a quick role change without any of the obligations that went with the job. Cora had eschewed marriage because it did not suit her needs and nature, yet she could not cope with the clichéd image her single state conveys. Like most "Closet Singles," she is torn between the desire to conform and the need to be different. So she tortures herself with the usual "Closet Single" self-flagellation behavior of setting up impossible standards for a marriage partner and then agonizing over her inability to find him.

It takes a tremendous amount of self-awareness and courage to kick over cultural stereotypes set down by society and your mother. But as more and more young women are doing it, older women should be encouraged to be single if they choose.

NO WOMAN SHOULD ever feel she has to conceal her wish to not marry from herself or anyone else. Nor should she be made to feel guilty because she has chosen to take a life route that has not been prescribed as regular and average. We live in a wonderfully free era when everyone is coming out of the closet and all sorts of behavior and lifestyles are being accepted, condoned, and even commended. Being single is not unnatural—if it works for you, it's wonderful.

Freedom is a system based on courage.
—Charles Péguy

13

THE MYTH OF POOR AUNT MARTHA

THE MYTH OF Maiden Aunts:
"Let's ask poor Aunt Martha to Christmas. She's all alone—you know, she's never been married"

So the pathetic, lonely aunt arrives in her new car wearing designer clothes bearing armloads of gifts for her great nieces and nephews, has a wonderful time, and goes home to her quiet and elegantly furnished condo leaving her harried niece to put five screaming children to bed and straighten up the mess in her cramped split-level living room after which she falls into an exhausted sleep ready to be up at six-thirty to prepare breakfast for seven people, make the beds, clean the bathrooms, and start thinking about lunch.

WHO'S TO BE PITIED HERE?

THE UNMARRIED OLDER woman has always been regarded as a sad figure whom we view sympathetically with just a touch of condescension. After all, she's a reject doomed to live outside of the normal mainstream of family life. She'll always be an invited guest, an appendage, but never really an integral part of the proceedings. Of course, she had her chances (a favorite family allegation to mitigate the premise that this female relative is not a total disaster), but she never had what it takes to persuade any man to choose her for his wife. Such a pity, she would have made a wonderful mother and helpmeet.

The presumption is always that the unmarried woman was unwanted and would certainly have chosen matrimony if only given the opportunity.

Contrast this dismal portrait with that of bachelor Uncle Joe, the same age as Martha, and doesn't he cut a dashing figure? Why Joe could charm the birds out of the trees. He's out with a different woman every night, he plays the field, does jaunty Joe. He'll never marry. He buys a new car every two years, wears expensive clothes, has a loft in Soho, is welcomed at every family celebration, and regarded with admiration tinged with envy.

Roget's Thesaurus' synonyms for unmarried man are bachelor and misogynist, meaning one who hates women, indicating a fellow who has deliberately avoided tying himself up with the disliked species. There is no such parallel synonym for an unmarried woman. All she can be called is spinster or old maid. There is no word to indicate her state could in any way be connected to choice.

But wasn't it? Isn't it time we looked back and started to reevaluate the position and motivations of unmarried aunts and those cousins and "courtesy cousins" who have been so misread? Substitute the name Martha for Joe in the above profiles, and it would play just as well. Perhaps all those single schoolteachers our mothers remember from childhood were more to be praised than pitied. Conceivably, they viewed marriage and all its concomitant benefits and drawbacks and decided that the negatives outweighed the positives and made the calculated courageously nonconformist choice to not marry.

In the 1920s and 1930s, the school systems were filled with spinster schoolteachers who were regarded as forbidding, but pathetic. Every respectful and slightly scared pupil's mother who was summoned before them could relieve her tension by feeling smug because after all, she had a husband and children while this pitiful woman could not even get herself a man. Let's review the realities of that era and see who was the one to be pitied.

THE SINGLE ESCAPE FROM DRUDGERY

ETHEL WAS THE fifth of eleven children living in a crowded two-bedroom apartment with one bathroom. Her parents were Irish immigrants who slept on a couch in the living room while the children crammed into the bedrooms. Ethel was a good student and somehow always managed to find a corner in which to do her homework. Although her mother barely had time to glance at her report card when she signed it, Ethel agonized over any mark below A. She adored and admired her teachers and was secretly determined to become one.

As she grew up, she saw her older sisters marrying and having babies immediately. She went out with boys, but school was her major interest, and the family laughingly called her "the little bookworm." Unlike some of her elder siblings, Ethel finished high school and then announced to everyone's shock that she was going on to college. There were many free tuition schools available in the area to young women who had the marks to qualify, and

Ethel did. Because her financial contribution to the family was needed, she worked evenings and weekends all through college.

Her sisters and mother could not understand Ethel. "You're going to get married and have kids anyway, so why do you want to go to college? Go to secretarial school, get a nice office job so you can make good money until you get married. College is a waste of time for girls." But it was her time and her decision.

After college, Ethel got a job as an elementary-school teacher in another neighborhood and shocked her family by announcing that she was moving into her own apartment. Ethel hated to make her parents unhappy, and she used as her main argument that she would need room to mark papers and do lesson preparation. Where would she do it in the crowded apartment with all those noisy younger brothers and sisters running about? She was finally able to get her parents' consent when she found an apartment in a woman's residence that conveyed the cachet of respectability her family could accept.

Ethel moved into the apartment and was absolutely ecstatic. For the first time in her life, she had her own space, privacy, and her own bathroom. She wallowed in the joys of furnishing it to her own taste. She loved the pleasure of eating alone, doing what she wanted and when she wanted. She went out to dinner and theater with friends and developed an active social life. There were boyfriends who took her dancing, to the movies, and sometimes on full-day outings that were fun.

She loved her work, she enjoyed her independence and ability to indulge herself and buy luxuries. It was heady stuff, and her mother's continual reminders that she was getting on in years and had better find a husband fast were falling on her progressively deafer ears.

Ethel went to family functions and saw her sisters' lives of virtual slavery as they cooked, cleaned, and cared for a growing stream of children. She enjoyed the hectic get-togethers and sharing the love and affection of the burgeoning brood, but she was glad to get home to her peaceful enclave and back to her very satisfying life.

Then her current boyfriend asked her to marry him. Ethel was surprised by her own reaction. Every young woman is primed for the joy of the big moment when she gets her proposal of marriage. It is the culmination of every little girl's dreams and the time when she can run to her mother and say proudly, "I did it!"

Yet Ethel felt no exhilaration and instead was troubled. She pleaded for time to give him her answer and did not mention his proposal to her mother because she knew that the family would pressure her to say "yes." Indeed, they would regard her as a lunatic if she said anything else. He had talked about wanting to take care of her and protect her, and she thought, "Protect me from what?" The days of dragons are over, and she was coping with life's vicissitudes extremely well all by herself. "Take care of her?" Didn't that actually mean having her take care of him, running his household, doing his laundry?

SHE DID NOT need him for support. In fact, she had a better income, job, and financial security than he did. So what beneficial life change was he offering? She saw the drudgery that women were committed to in marriage and contrasted it to her own lovely, orderly existence. Of what would she be deprived if she said "no"? True, she would probably not see him anymore, but although she liked him very much, it was not an overpowering passion, and she could live without him.

If she chose to eschew marriage altogether, she would be giving up motherhood. But she had grown up in a large family and already had twenty-three nieces and nephews. True, they were not her children, but then, they were also not her responsibility.

Ethel thanked him very much and said "no" as she did to the few subsequent proposals received from other suitors. As the years passed, she traveled every summer and saw every part of the world. She moved ahead in her career and became the principal of her school, a position she thoroughly enjoyed. When Christmas came, she always managed to spend the holidays with some of her nieces and nephews.

"Of course we'll ask your poor Aunt Ethel. After all, the sad little thing has no family of her own."

IT IS TIME for a revisionist view of the history of maiden aunts and spinsters, these much maligned women portrayed in literature as sad creatures who are slightly dotty and usually eccentric bordering on imbecility. Even Miss Jane Marple, Agatha Christie's famed maiden sleuth, although exhibiting the brains to solve thorny mysteries, is portrayed as a provincial "pussy" as the English refer to an unmarried lady of advanced years and slightly diminished capacity.

The presupposition that all such women were left unmarried because no men found them desirable is ludicrous. How many of these women made value judgments about the benefits of marriage and merely decided against it—and chose to take no husband? Given the subordinate position of wives years ago, both socially and legally, their choice was intelligent and courageous. They risked ridicule, being the butt of barbs of crude men who treated them with condescension. They risked being viewed as socially crippled because they were assumed to be virgins who are terminally deprived of the transcendent experience of sexual intercourse and, therefore, according to Dr. Freud, destined to go through life embittered and frustrated.

They risked being regarded in many ways as second-class citizens of the world...and yet they made the choice. These women opted to be single in a world of marrieds. Their acts of self-determination took the kind of guts and strength of character that should forever erase the epithets of "timid," "pathetic," and "pitiful" as applied to maiden aunts.

14

WOMEN EMPOWERED TO BE FREE:

LETTERS FROM READERS OF WHY WOMEN SHOULDN'T MARRY

T HE MOST GRATIFYING thing for an author is to know she has touched people's lives. If she's lucky, some readers let her know how her book has helped them.

Since the first edition of *Why Women Shouldn't Marry* was published in 1988, Cynthia has received many letters and e-mails from women who wanted to express their gratitude for how deeply the book changed their approach to life. In some cases, the book helped them understand and feel justified for having made life-changing choices.

Why Women Shouldn't Marry was translated into Japanese and published in Japan, a country that is undergoing dramatic social change as women are rejecting traditional subservient roles.

In October of 2007, while this edition was being written, Cynthia received an e-mail from a Japanese reader, which we have included here along with just some of the other letters that prove the important truths set forth in *Why Women Shouldn't Marry* are as valid today as then. Some of the experiences described may well mirror yours and other women's throughout the world. We think you will be inspired by their letters and hope they will help you find the solutions you seek.

October 2007—Japan

Dear Ms. Smith,

At first, please forgive my any mistakes in my English.

Hello, Ms Smith. I am a woman who lives in…in Japan. I am forty-two years old. I have just read your book *Why Women Shouldn't Marry*. I haven't known that such a great book like this had published for almost twenty years ago.

I married when I was thirty-seven, and divorced two years ago. He was four-year older than me. If I could have read your book when I was about to marry, I am sure I could have a second thought.

When we just married, my husband said like this, "I love you and respect you, because you always know what you do and what you want. You have your own career, and love your job. I want to join and support your dream."

Soon after married, we had to live with his parents. His parents were physically very healthy and they had enough money. So they didn't need our any help. But they insisted that this is a traditional Japanese way to live with your own son and his family. You might not believe this, but it is not unusual situation in Japan. My husband never said "No" to his parents in his life. That was a big shock to me.

Because he was strong and outgoing in front of people all the time. He said "Quit your job. I want you to stay home and spend time with my parents while I am at work." The worst part was, his parents and all relatives thought that it was a shame that his wife had her own job.

In Japan, there is people who think like this "His wife is working? He can't afford to support his family." But I couldn't give up my job. I wanted him to understand me. And I thought he will if I try hard. So I tried to do housework completely and took care of his parents, while continued working.

He kept accusing me and my work. In the end, when my salary became bigger than his, he was furious at me. We had same kind of job. We worked for a publishing company. He was an advertising director, and I was a copy writer. Whenever I was hearing him complaining about me, I couldn't help thinking this way, "Why he doesn't happy about my success at all...Is he jealous?"

Now I am single again, and am working all day. Sometimes it is hard to live alone in Japan, especially woman at my age. But I never want to marry again! Never!

Because at least my life became more interesting and predictable. I am incredibly happier now. In my life, my precious things are my humorous mother, my intelligent girlfriends, my best-friend sister, and her adorable two-year-old son.

I want to say thank you very much, Mis Smith. Your book made me notice, cry, and gave me courage.

Some of my friends have the similar situation with their husbands. They don't love their partner anymore. But they can't leave them for many reason. I think I recommend your book to them.

I am very very happy if you read my e-mail. I am sorry again for my poor English.

Please take care of yourself, Mis Smith. Thank you so much for giving me encouragement and hope to live.

NK

February 1989—Korea

I bought your book *Why Women Shouldn't Marry* for its title at the U.S. Army bookstore in Seoul. But after reading it, I couldn't help but feel that I had to write to you and let you know what a wonderful book it is and the inspiration it has given me!

I'm a 41-year-old management assistant working for the U.S. Army in Korea. At the moment I'm going through a very rough divorce after 16 years of marriage. For the past months, I'd been living in a very stressful situation. I was having nightmares, couldn't sleep or eat. I felt like a failure and blamed myself for everything. I couldn't accept the fact that my marriage was over. It hurt so much at times that I was even thinking about committing suicide.

Then I found your book. It gave me the strength that I thought I never had before. With your encouragement in the book, I realize that it's OK to get a divorce and strike out on my own, rather than living in a suffocating and stressful marriage. I've read your book over and over, especially when I'm feeling depressed—it has become my close friend and confidante. Cynthia, it's so comforting to know that there is someone out there that understands you, knowing what you're going through and told you that you'll be OK, that there is life after divorce, that you're better off without him and that you can have a new life, perhaps even more exciting.

Cynthia, thank you so much for writing this lifesaving book. You certainly have saved my life. I wish you much more success in your wonderful work. May God bless you always.

Sincerely yours,
JR

July 1989—Texas

After reading your book *Why Women Shouldn't Marry* I now have a clear picture of myself. I just can't believe how willing I was all my life to give myself over for someone to protect me. So much energy has been exhausted in that eternal search for Mr. Right. I think I was always looking for myself in others and now realize that if I had concentrated on what I really wanted I would have realized that I didn't need to be married.

I have been married twice and did not like what I got from it either time. Since reading your book I have had peace of mind and I can't believe how much energy I now have. My life was a complete struggle for identity and purpose and I feel certain now that it was all based on the fact that I was raised to believe that I would have to marry in order to complete my life.

I thank you for writing this book and would like you to know that it has helped at least one person and I'm sure many others.

Yours truly,
TJ

September 1989—Wisconsin

Your book *Why Women Shouldn't Marry* said it all. I am a 50-year-old divorced woman of nine years and was raised during a generation where women got married and had babies shortly after graduating from high school.

In the first 35 years of my life I thought my father was "God"—he was ruler of the house. For 21 years of my life I was married to a man who I thought could walk on water. It took me two years to decide on a divorce. My sons were grown by that time. The greatest incentive I have ever received to succeed as a happy and prosperous single I owe to my ex-husband. I can still see him in the courtroom yelling at me and shaking his finger in my face yelling "You will never make it without me."

I worked two jobs after relocating. I trained in data processing and worked part time as a desk clerk in a motel. In 1981, I purchased my first new car with my own credit. In 1982, I purchased a 40-year-old-ranch house which I love with all my heart. This was done with MY credit. In the past 9 years I have vacationed in Arizona and Florida, gone white water rafting, etc.

I have found that men do not have the support system that single women do. Women can talk to women about anything. Men cannot talk to men about anything. I do not like the person I was when I was married. I do like myself now. I never fully understood why I stayed married so long or why I have stayed single since my divorce until I read your book.

Thank you for writing *Why Women Shouldn't Marry*. I could not grow until I got my divorce. Your book is true to fact. God bless you.

Sincerely,
CB

April 1991—Illinois

My husband and I, both 71 years old, after 46 years of marriage, 5 lovely well-educated children, decided to split. No attorneys, no divorce—just living apart. Our marriage was intolerable. He and my son helped me find and move into a pleasant apartment on Lake Michigan.

My problem was—how would I like this setup. I was recovering from a deep depression. Now what?

Almost four years have passed. I've never been so happy. I am "Me." My apartment is just the way I like it. My schedule is mine. All kinds of opportunities have opened up. I travel extensively. I don't have to get anybody's approval. Our children feel good about our arrangement. My health, now at 75, is excellent.

Your wonderful book answered so many questions. Thank you.

Sincerely,
SR

August 1989—New Jersey

I've just finished reading your new book and with sadness I feel I'm saying goodbye to a friend. Oh how timely those words are to me. Although in the Black community, a Black woman who is attractive is not allowed to have a man. I don't want any romantic relationships.

Keeping my freedom is a daily battle.

I felt alone for so long in my conclusions about marriage. Then you came along with an eloquent affirmation of what I secretly believe to be true. I saw you on "Oprah" and was annoyed at how some of those women tried to put words into your mouth.

You probably know little about my culture, but if you believe that White women have few advantages, a Black woman has none. If by chance a Black man has a good paying job that means the woman has no rights at all within the marriage. For he is seen as a rarity, a high premium product—it's downright disgusting.

I really enjoyed your book. It isn't often that a woman sees things as they really are.

Sincerely,
HT

Words, words, words.
—WILLIAM SHAKESPEARE, HAMLET

15

YOU'RE NOT UNMARRIED...
YOU'RE SINGLE

SINGLE IS NO longer singular. It's a whole new frame of reference. It's a whole new frame of mind. If being married is becoming no longer the norm, then it stands to reason that not being married is no longer abnormal. So get it out of your head that you are in any way different or need to be defensive about the fact that you are a single person. Leave that to your mother.

Just because she has her mother-of-the-bride dress hanging in the closet is no reason for you to be apologetic for being what you are and choose to be...single.

This does not require that you make a public proclamation and get a bumper sticker that says "Single is Special." Being single is not a cause, an occupation, or even a permanent condition. It is the way you choose to live now. You may find someone you wish to marry at some point, who knows? But looking for a husband should not be your obsessive goal, and you should not spend your life in a holding pattern.

In other words, you are not looking, you are living. You are not a woman who is waiting to be married, you are a person who is single.

Free yourself of the compulsion to read those books that tell you how to land a husband and demean you into feeling like a reject. Why make yourself into one of those desperate souls seeking the elusive Mr. Right?

An article in the September 27, 2007, Style Section of the *New York Times* describes a new growth industry called "Dating Coaches." The coaches' sole goal is to teach you how to date and how to behave to become more alluring or at least acceptable to the opposite sex.

According to the article, most of the clients are women in their twenties and thirties who devote fifteen hours a week to their search at the rate of $125 per hour; some have been known to have spent thousands of dollars. If you think this is just one of those flash-in-the-pan businesses started by canny opportunists, you may be surprised to learn that they have taken themselves seriously enough to have formed their own trade association, the International Coach Federation. Qualifications for membership? Who knows? Since they do not get you dates or offer guarantees of any kind, caveat emptor seems to be a given.

The only issue here is what if they are successful and as a result of their coaching, the guy succumbs to your unnaturally induced charms and marries you? You have spent a fortune learning how to be someone other than yourself, so now what happens? When you relax and become "you" again, does he learn he has married a stranger and want out, or do you become a "Stepford Wife"?

Don't let desperation drive you to unlivable lengths. Don't let comments from unthinking idiots affect you. Ignore those crude idiots who ask if you're married yet. The real problem is theirs, not yours.

Enjoy your achievements, your career, your independence, and don't let anyone push you into an "until" life that is a throwback to those days when it was a given that a woman worked (at secretarial, typist, and other nonexecutive jobs) until she got married. Live your full life happily and serenely as a single person, and if you should happen to come across a man who you think would enrich your life and whom you wish to marry, great. Should you wish to continue forever as you are, also great.

YOU ARE NOT ALONE IN BEING SINGLE ANYMORE

"51% OF WOMEN Are Now Living Without Spouse" is the headline of a front-page article in the January 16, 2007 issue of the *New York Times*. The question posed is how do you think this trend will shape social and workplace policies?

One very apparent area that shows significant change is in the marketplace. Singles are now recognized as having an impact on the American and global economies. A topic high on the agenda at the 2007 World Economic Forum held in Davos, Switzerland, was "the Singles Economy."

We can no longer be ignored, but rather have become prime consumer desirables. Currently, compiled statistics indicate that singles have now become a vital force in purchasing power throughout the world.

What does this mean to us? The late comedian Rodney Dangerfield used to complain, "I can't get no respect." That used to apply to single people in restaurants, hotels, and other places where service to singles was definitely second rate. Rejoice...we've now reached the front of the line.

All major marketers are being given a heads-up to aim their advertising toward this growing group of consumers who now are leading the buying market, replacing married couples in their forties and fifties. The federal government estimates that single consumers contribute $1.6 trillion to the economy. If Madison Avenue loves us—we are definitely "In."

A report titled "Singles In The U.S.: The New Nuclear Family" was compiled by Packaged Facts, a division of marketresearch.com. The report examined the attitudes of today's single consumers including never-married, divorced, and widowed adults, which they claim now accounts for a majority of American households.

"People are single today because they increasingly choose to be. The days of the pathetic single sitting all alone at home moping over his or her lonely existence are over," said Tatjiana Meerman, managing editor of their report.

If you need further confirmation that you are not alone being single, the Census Bureau showed that as of 2000, the most common household in the U.S. is people living alone; 27 million households, compared with 25 million consisting of husband, wife, and child.

Once Madison Avenue has verified our value, can the media be far behind? Apparently not. Here are newspapers that considered the fantastic growth of single people a trend worthy of news stories that appeared between 2005 and 2007:

"Alone no more. Singles fight for their rights"
Orlando Sentinel; Naples Daily News; St. Louis Post-Dispatch;
The Ledger, Lakeland, FL; Winston-Salem (NC) Journal

"With so many singles in U.S. you'd expect fairer treatment"
Everett (WA) Daily Herald

"One: it's no longer the loneliest number"

Dayton Daily News

"Satisfyingly Single"

Duluth News Tribune

"Interest groups for Singles are on the rise"

Staten Island (NY) *Advance*

"Me, myself and I"

Chicago Courier News

"Single Minded"

Boston Globe

"Single households now a majority"

Clinton (OK) *Herald; Daily Times,* Prior, OK

Andy Rooney, the elder statesman of CBS's "60 Minutes," has noted the change this way: "For every stunning, smart, well-coiffed hot woman over forty, there is a bald, paunchy relic in yellow pants making a fool of himself with some twenty-two-year-old waitress. Ladies, I apologize. For all those men who say, "Why buy a cow when you can get the milk for free," here's an update for you. Nowadays, 80 percent of women are against marriage. Why? Because women realize it's not worth buying an entire pig to get a little sausage!"

THE ERA OF CHOICE

THERE IS NO longer any need for apologias, explanations, self-doubts, or sadness because you are not something that others expect you to be. If you have found that you like living as a single person, keep right on going. If you decide to have a child and be a single mother, go ahead.

These are your choices and should not be judged by the way others have opted to live. Look around you, and listen. There is no longer any better or worse way to live, only different. It is time to accept yourself happily for what and who you are and not identify yourself by what you are not.

You no longer have to explain yourself, excuse your status, or be made to feel in any way deprived or inferior because you have chosen not to marry. Relax, rejoice, and enjoy the freedom to be you.